# SPECIALIST MILITARY AIRCRAFT

SPECIALIST MILITARY AIRCRAFT

# SPECIALIST MILITARY AIRCRAFT

SPECIALIST MILITARY AIRCRAFT

Octavio Díez

**UDYAT**

Author
Octavio Díez

Collection Design
S. García

Editorial Co-ordination
E. Marín

Editorial project
2006 © UDYAT S.L.

ISBN: 84-934728-1-6
Legal deposit: B-20601/2006

Printed in Spain

# SPECIALIST MILITARY AIRCRAFT

## INDEX

# EADS/CASA
## TRANSPORT AIRCRAFT

Several years ago, various European countries decided to merge their civil and military aviation industries, creating a group called EADS (European Aeronautic Defence and Space), which also included the Spanish company Construcciones Aeronáuticas S.A. (CASA).

As a result of this merger, a range of light and medium transport planes is being sold, based on Spain's most emblematic aircraft designs. This range of aircraft has been very successful in recent decades, and more than seven hundred units have been sold.

**Light and efficient**

The thirtieth anniversary of the first flight of the C-212 light transport plane, called the Aviocar, was celebrated in 2001. This has been a great commercial success, as there are currently more than four hundred and seventy examples serving with airforces and commercial airlines in more than forty countries and being used for a wide variety of

tasks. As proof of the quality and productivity of this model, it has already exceeded two and a half million flying-hours, with a very low accident rate.

Important features of the C-212 are its robustness, reliability, ease of operation and maintenance, and a multi-role capability much favoured by civilian companies and military operators. Amongst the latter, are various specialised squadrons belonging to the air forces of countries such as Thailand, Venezuela, Uruguay, Panama, Mexico, Bolivia, Colombia, Chile, France, Indonesia and Ireland, with the Portuguese and the Jordanians being the first to take an interest in the Aviocar.

Basically, this model is characterised by its

fixed landing gear, designed to operate from improvised, or earth landing-strips; its high wing, which gives it the ability to take-off or land in very short spaces without interfering with its load-carrying capacity; and its two low-consumption engines. The cockpit for two pilots is sited at the front of the fuselage, with the majority given over to carrying all types of cargo, from twenty-five paratroops to three tonnes of equipment, although there are limits defined by the access area, and the capacity of the ramp. The first models to enter service were followed by the 100, 200, 300 and 400 series, the latter being presented at Paris in June 1997. The use of advanced technology, particularly as far as the cockpit

is concerned, and the improvement in its aerodynamic properties when flying at low altitude, have led to the development of different versions, with improved capabilities. For example, the latest production models have a transport capacity in excess of four hundred kilograms, thanks to the installation of Allied Signal TPE-331-12JR-710C engines, which each provide an extra 925 horsepower, and which have led to improved take-off performance, and the ability to fly at very high ambient temperatures.

Taking the standard model as the base, various versions have been designed to satisfy a greater number of users. Some have been modified for VIP transport, others have been fitted with electronic intelligence-gathering systems, and several have been converted for maritime reconnaissance or for search and rescue services.

### Greater Potential

In 1979, the success obtained with the C-212 Aviocar, encouraged the Spanish at CASA to form a partnership with Nurtanio of Indonesia to design and manufacture a more capable model, a plane which received the designation CN-235, although friction between the two companies meant that each one built it independently of the other. This design has been used by the Thai Police in an auxiliary role, and for casualty evacuation by the Turkish Air Force (TUAF), which installed 12 beds and 2 field surgeries in its cargo-bay. The French

Air Mobility Command used it for tactical and logistics transport during Operation Turquoise in Rwanda, and the Irish Air Corps have used it for fishery protection.

It has carried out many other duties with the air forces of various countries including Spain, Brunei, Colombia, Chile, Ecuador, Botswana, Gabon, Morocco, Panama, Papua New Guinea, Saudi Arabia and the United Arab Emirates. The latest customer is the United States Coast Guard, which has just ordered two CN-235M MPA.

To date, two hundred and fifty CN-235s have been sold, but the model has not been assigned an official identifying name. From 1983, the year in which the first prototypes were presented, to the present day, users

have accumulated more than six hundred and fifty thousand flying hours, which shows a high level of operability.

The first models were followed by the series 10, 100 and 300, with the letter M being assigned to those versions destined for military use, which differentiates them from those assigned to less arduous tasks. Its most appreciated qualities include the capability of transporting 36 paratroops 1,650 km from their base; the ability to evacuate 21 wounded from a place 2,370 km away from the departure point; the ability to search for naval targets for nine hours, at a distance of 170 km from base, and being able to move 2 tonnes of cargo 2,340 km, in all cases whilst being able to return to the departure point.

This good performance is due to an exceptional payload to structural weight ratio - compound materials were used in manufacture, and the incorporation of a low consumption, easy-to-maintain power plant. The plane features a rather spacious pressurised cabin, which allows a wide variety of cargo to be transported, always so long as this totals less than six tonnes. Furthermore, it is equipped with short, robust, landing-gear, with two low-pressure wheels in tandem, allowing it to operate from unpaved airfields, and a rear ramp with double doors which permits rapid loading of personnel and light vehicles.

The wings are sited above the hold, and contain the two main and two auxiliary fuel tanks, which have a total capacity of 5,268 litres and are fitted with two gravity-fed and one pressure-fed filling-points. The tanks feed the power-plant comprising two General Electric CT7-9C turbo-props, which turn four-bladed Hamilton Standard 14RF-21 propellers and have a take-off thrust of 1,750 horsepower. More developed versions have been derived from the standard transport model, notably the Persuader. This is a specialised platform for maritime surveillance and patrol missions,

fitted with a Litton APS504 search radar below the fuselage, an optronic infra-red detection system integrated with the primary radar, for optimum search and identification, and a console for the systems operator. Advantage has been taken of this experience, and the subsequent sales, to produce a specialised maritime patrol version which includes CASA's FITS system (Fully Integrated Tactical System), which has improved features.

**New markets**

The search for more customers, and the Spanish air force requirement for a new transport plane of greater capacity than previous models, led CASA to develop the C-295, a model derived from the CN-235, although notably more capable.

Use has been made of the basic design, and the fuselage has been enlarged, to obtain a load capacity 50% greater in terms of weight, than its predecessor. Range has also been increased, by combining an increase in the fuel capacity with the fitting of an in-flight refuelling probe. Maximum cruise speed has also increased to 480 kilometres per hour while, at the same time, the latest technology

has been applied to achieve a considerable reduction in costs over the life-cycle of the plane.

The C-295, already bought by Abu Dhabi, Brazil, Spain, Jordan and Poland, has been flying since 1998, and the first production models began to be delivered in 2001. The unique capabilities of this very versatile model include the ability to transport up to seventy-five soldiers, five 108"x 88" containers, three fighter-bomber jet engines or three Land Rover type light vehicles, whilst maintaining the robust design and STOL ability of its smaller brothers. Similarly, the ample hold can be adapted to various tasks, from anti-submarine patrol to reconnaissance, if fitted with the appropriate sensors. Its dimensions include a length of 24.50 m and a wing-span of 25.81 m. Maximum take-off weight can exceed twenty-three tons, although it normally flies at twenty-one; the 9,250 litres of fuel in its tanks give it a range in excess of five thousand six hundred kilometres. All these characteristics mean that this model has a bright future ahead, with various countries, including Australia, showing an interest in purchasing it.

## Technical details C212 Series 400

| | |
|---|---|
| **Cost (in millions of dollars):** | 13 |
| **Size:** | |
| Length | 16,15 m |
| Height | 6,59 m |
| Wingspan | 20,27 m |
| Wing area | 41,00 m² |
| Flap area | 7,47 m² |
| **Weight:** | |
| Empty | 3.800 kg |
| Maximum | 8.100 kg |
| Maximum load | 2.950 kg |
| Fuel | 2.040 l |
| **Engines:** | 2 Allied-Signal TPE-331-12-JR-701C turboprops with 925 continuous horsepower |
| **Performance:** | |
| Ceiling | 7.925 m |
| Maximum speed | 354 km/h |
| Take-off requirement | 384 m in STOL operations |
| Maximum range | 2,680 km reducing to 835 km on military operations fully loaded |

## Technical details: CN-235M

| | |
|---|---|
| **Cost (in millions of dollars):** | 16 |
| **Size:** | |
| Length | 21,40 m |
| Altura | 8,17 m |
| Wingspan | 25,81 m |
| Wing area | 59,10 m² |
| Flap area | 10,87 m² |
| **Weight:** | |
| Military version, unladen | 8.800 kg |
| Maximum | 16.500 kg |
| Maximum load | 6.000 kg |
| Fuel | 5.268 l |
| **Engines:** | 2 Allied-Signal TPE-331-12-JR-701C turboprops with 925 continuous horsepower |
| **Performance:** | |
| Ceiling | 8.230 m |
| Cruising speed | 445 km/h |
| Minimum speed | 156 km/h with flaps down |
| Take-off requirement | 512 m |
| Landing distance | 376 m |
| Maximum range | 1.500 km with 6 t of cargo or 4.450 km with 3,55 t |

# A400M,
## THE EUROPEAN STRATEGIC CHALLENGE

The conflicts which have broken out at the start of the 21st century, and operations where it has been necessary to send humanitarian aid by air, have shown European countries that they lack a real strategic transport capability. This has obliged them to charter large-capacity Russian aircraft, or to ask for US help, in order to participate in various operations.

Apart from other reasons, such as the need to replace aging fleets of planes like the C-160 Transall or the C-130 Hercules, which are used by many countries, this reality has encouraged the birth of a Europe-wide international programme to try and produce a new transport plane, much more capable than those it will replace. This is the model which has been designated generically the A400M, and which, for the moment, does not have a name. Basically the concept is the same as the design which was previously known by the initials FLA, or Future Large Aircraft.

**A joint effort**
To reach the production stage, the initial design has been through a long, and sometimes problematic, process. Back in 1993, seven countries signed an agreement committing them to join forces to develop the FLA. Specifically, the group consisted of Germany, Belgium, Spain, France, Italy, Turkey and the UK, with Italy finally deciding to leave, and Luxembourg and Portugal joining later. Financial problems led to the Portuguese abandoning their plans to buy three of these aircraft.

Discussions between these countries led to a long gestation period before it was finally ready for production, as many factors – among them, political, industrial and financial have been considered – apart from

◁ *Fitting a fixed probe is planned, enabling it to receive fuel from other planes in flight, including from those of the same type, to guarantee an extensive operating range.*

▲ *Each A400M can carry over a hundred paratroops. Half-a-dozen planes can carry a battalion in one sortie, and a brigade over several.*

the purely military. The first operational aircraft are not expected to be delivered until the end of this decade, and the date of the maiden flight of the first prototype has been fixed for 2008. At present, apart from a planning model that has allowed the general dimensions and validity of the project to be confirmed, all that has been decided is that the programme will be controlled by Airbus Military, a Madrid-based subsidiary of Airbus Industries. Additionally, there are other companies which are directly, or indirectly, involved in the planning and manufacturing process, such as the UK's BAe systems, the multinational company EADS, the Belgian Flabel, and the Turkish Tusas Aerospace Industries.

This framework of companies, including those mentioned above and many more, will be in charge of manufacturing components and equipment in accordance with a dis-

tribution of tasks and percentages based on the number of planes ordered by each country. The final assembly process and test flights will be carried out at a refurbished site which EADS/CASA is preparing in Seville. Spain's participation in this programme will lead to an additional benefit in the shape of the expansion of its industrial fabric in the aerospace sector and the associated jobs which will be created. The A400M programme is overseen at management level by the European OCCAR agency (Organisation Conjointe de Coopération en Matière d'Armement - Organisation for Joint Armament Co-operation), although it is the various national governments which have exercised the greatest pressure to continue a project which has frequently been in doubt. The definitive wording of this multinational contract took shape on the 27th May 2003 and, as a result, twenty thousand million

euros will be invested to buy one hundred and eighty planes, the largest defence contract in history.

The initial purchase plans include sixty for Germany, fifty for France, twenty-seven for Spain, twenty-five for the UK, ten for Turkey, seven for Belgium and one for Luxembourg.

**Important features**

The majority of the A400M transport planes will be delivered in the second decade of this century, and possible future customers such as Australia or Canada are already being considered, although there is no firm news in this respect. What all the users are interested in is the real performance, that is to say, the ability to carry a maximum load of thirty-seven tonnes in its hold or to move armoured vehicles or other heavy equipment which, due to its weight or size, does not fit in the planes which will be replaced.

With a twenty tonne load, which is more than the C-130's maximum, it can cover a distance of roughly five thousand kilometres at maximum cruising speed. Its design as a strategic transport makes it easy to convert for other missions, such as in-flight refuelling, and it can also accommodate up to one hundred and twenty fully-equipped men. Some of the features worth mentioning are that it has been designed to be able to take-off and land in areas which lack infrastructure, such as short runways or even roads; that it has internal fittings for a 5 tonne crane to help move loads; and that it can receive fuel in-flight. It also features reduced operating costs, which should fall dramatically during its useful life, which will be around thirty years, depending on the operational handling received.

One of its interesting features is its ability to maintain a high cruising speed. This is due to the aerodynamic efficiency of the fuselage and the wing as much as to the power of the four turbo-props with eight-bladed propellers.

The cockpit, which seats two pilots, is equipped with the most up-to-date data presentation display screens to reduce their workload. It is also worth pointing out that the equipment is totally compatible with night vision systems and that it is fitted with the same fly-by-wire flight control system fitted to Airbus' civilian planes. Self-defence has been ensured by providing it with detectors, launchers for flares and chaff, and the installation of a Northrop Grumman AN/APN-241E navigation radar.

| Technical details: A400M* | |
|---|---|
| **Cost (in millions of dollars):** | 112 |
| **Size:** | |
| Length | 42,20 m |
| Height | 14,70 m |
| Wingspan | 42,40 m |
| Wing area | 221,50 m² |
| **Weight** | |
| Empty | 66.500 kg |
| Maximum | 130.000 kg |
| Maximum load | 37.000 kg |
| Internal load | 50.000 l |
| **Engines:** | Four TP400-D6 turbofans, with 11,000 horsepower thrust each |
| **Performance:** | |
| Ceiling | 11.277 m |
| Maximum speed | 780 km/h |
| Take-off requirement | 900 m |
| Maximum range | 8.000 km |
| | (*) planned, not definitive details. |

# THE C-130
## HERCULES

Air forces all over the world have appreciated the Hercules' transport capacity, versatility and reliability. This American aircraft has been a great international success, having sold more than two thousand two hundred examples.

◣ One of the missions this plane is used for is the resupply of personnel carrying out scientific missions in the Antarctic, which requires it to land on ice.

▶ The cockpit for the flight crew of the C-130 is situated in an elevated position so that the pilots enjoy good all-round vision, which is vital in transport missions.

In years to come, it is hoped that this figure will increase significantly, as many operators, including the US Air Force, will need to renew their fleets of outdated C-130s.

Its design is conventional, but it boasts an enviable adaptability. There are examples in service as cargo-carriers, but they have also been modified to carry out in-flight refuelling missions, airborne early warning, search and rescue (SAR), fire-support to suppress ground targets, electronic warfare, photo-reconnaissance, and many other missions depending on operator requirements, both civilian and military.

### A pleasant surprise

Currently, more than seventy countries have bought it to serve in their military air fleets, to which have to be added those employed by several civilian companies, who have also been

positively impressed by the services obtained using this extraordinary plane. Nobody could have imagined that this plane would still be in service after fifty years, yet the first of the prototypes built by Lockheed flew on August 23rd, 1954.

The performance of this first version was a notable improvement on the previous designs, above all for its ability to operate from semi-prepared airstrips, and because of its enormous rear door, which eased loading and unloading. These details, among others, led the US Air Force to sign an order for two hundred and thirty planes of the A version, which were all delivered before the end of the decade.

In June 1959, the B version was developed, which included more powerful engines and an increased fuel load, while the E version was ready in April 1962, with an increased maximum take-off weight and a 5,145 litre fuel tank in each wing. Exports began with the arrival of the H version in March 1965, which was notable for an increase in the useful load capacity to around nineteen tonnes of cargo or up to seventy paratroops.

The most recent development is the C-130J version, a model which started production in 1997 and entered service shortly afterwards, having already suffered some design setbacks which resulted in significant delays to the anticipated delivery schedule.

Despite this, its abilities had aroused wide-spread expectations, and nearly two hundred have already been purchased by Australia, Denmark, the USA, UK, Italy and Kuwait; some of these countries opted for the standard version, while others have ordered it as a variant with a longer fuselage, designated the CC-130J. As a result, this variant has a larger hold, and a longer range.

**Service possibilities**

Its versatility has been put to the test in many conflicts over the last four decades, but above all during Operation Desert Shield in 1990, in which its transport ability answered the challenge of supplying and resupplying materiel and moving troops. At the same time, it has played a key role in humanitarian support missions.

In addition to this basic mission, that of transporting any load which fits in its hold and which does not exceed the maximum author-

ised weight (ranging from light vehicles to containers fitted with air detection radars), there is the no less important one of moving troops, especially in airborne assault operations, or those involving dropping paratroops, whether they are mass assaults, or the insertion of small groups of special operations forces.

An example of this type of mission is one where fifteen or so commandos are transported to a point where they jump using manually-opening parachutes for accurate landing, or one where they use automatic opening to land in the water and subsequently recover the inflatable craft dropped with them. Apart from these basic activities, the C-130 has undergone a process of transformation unmatched, to date, by any other plane. One of the most eye-catching variants is the

AC-130 model which has various internal mountings for cannon and multi-barrelled machine-guns, which it can enables its enormous, deadly fire-power to be trained on ground targets. On this type of mission, the Hercules has to circle over a pre-determined area, concentrating its fire on one or more targets.

Another interesting model, designated the KC-130, is the conversion to an aerial refuelling tanker, with an extra fuel tank fitted inside the cargo bay. This is not strictly necessary, as it is already fitted with two tanks under the wings housing the refuelling probes. Both more expensive, and more complicated, is the EC-130 Compass Call, which is crammed full of electronic systems designed to interfere with the enemy's communications and ensure that his command and control systems

do not work properly. The MC-130 Combat Talon II is modified with all sorts of support equipment for special operations forces. Its adaptability allows it to be fitted with skids so that it can land in frozen areas, enabling stores to be transferred to Antarctic bases. A strange modification is known as Eagle Claw, which comprises auxiliary rockets fitted to the sides that enable it to take-off and land in spaces as small as a football field. This was developed for the attempted rescue of the American hostages held in Iran by Ayatollah Khomeini's regime.

All these versions have made use of the original design based on a medium transport of unparalleled performance, especially with regard to load carried and places of operation. Additionally, the fact that it is fitted with four engines for propulsion gives

it high levels of performance, as well as additional security, in case one of them fails. The normal crew comprises a pilot, co-pilot and navigator who travel in a raised cabin which boasts excellent visibility, supported by a further group of two or three crew who attend to the various sub-systems and the load.

## Upgraded performance

The arrival on the world market of the C-130J, now made by Lockheed Martin, has brought a future into perspective where one can imagine the Hercules flying until at least the middle of this century. This will be possible because the performance of the current version is much improved, above all as regards reliability, operating costs and ease of maintenance. It is also foreseeable that new versions will keep appearing or a decision will be made to upgrade the planes currently flying to the standard of the J model, as has already happened in recent years, in order to prolong an already long operating life.

The most important of the features which characterise the J version is the replacement of the engines. The power plant has been renewed and now consists of four powerful Rolls-Royce AE2100D3 turboprops. This engine is noteworthy, as it produces 4,591 horsepower of thrust per unit and uses a very advanced six-bladed scimitar propeller, made by Dowty Aerospace. These

▶ *The external details of the cockpit of the Hercules transport aircraft can be seen in this photo. The pilots have exceptional visibility and their position makes difficult landings easier.*

▼ *The hold of the Hercules is quite large which enables it to load bulky cargo. Cargo is limited by its size and weight and, above all, by the weight limits of the ramp.*

▶ ▶ *Dropping paratroops is one of the most frequent activities carried out by this transport plane. The men are normally seated in four rows they reach the drop-off zone.*

propellers are more efficient, leading to a substantial improvement in range and speed over previous versions.

Another important detail is the cockpit itself. It has been completely redesigned to incorporate the latest available technology, including LCD (Liquid Crystal Display) data presentation screens similar to those fitted to the latest fighter-bombers. They show both crew members the engine parameters, digital maps of the ground, and any information that might be required during the mission. Additionally, it was decided to fit holographic head-up displays, to avoid the pilots needing to move their eyes from their normal positions to learn relevant flight information.

Special attention has been paid to survivability both by applying armour to certain areas of the cabin and by fitting AN/AAR-47 self-defence sensors and AN/ALE-47 launchers, which can fire both infra-red flares and chaff. The USAF wants to improve this protection by installing the AN/AAQ-24(V) NEMESIS, a system which acts against infra-red threats, for example the heat-seeking warheads of short-range air-to-air missiles.

It includes an accurate navigation system based on GPS/IN, a meteorological and navigation radar, and an air-traffic system to warn of possible collisions: the SKE 2000 radar alerts the crew to the distance which separates them from the ground and to possible ground impacts, which makes it easier to fly at low level and dodge possible enemy anti-aircraft fire.

A roller-system has been fitted to the cargo-

bay floor, to ease the movement of loads, and it is extremely useful for cargo-drops over the target area. The plane's capacity, whether measured by volume or by weight, does not allow for the transport of tanks, but it can carry those light armoured vehicles which can fit inside; many of the more modern ones, such as the 8x8 Striker recently purchased by the US Army, have been designed to be able to be transported by the C-130J and previous models.

This new model also includes two mission computers linked by two-way data buses, which leads to duplication that enables it to function in the case of a breakdown. The system is designed to receive information from numerous sensors sited at various points around the fuselage, to advise the crew in case of any important failure which might need attention, and to provide the necessary correction: the equipment itself will help to solve the problem, using its self-diagnostic capability.

The plane's performance has also been notably improved. It can reach a higher altitude more rapidly and can take off and land in less distance than the previous versions. Its range can be extended by in-flight refuelling, meaning that it can take off with a full load and avoid the need to calculate the fuel required to carry the load to the final objective.

All of these features and the current and future order book mean that it is certain that the Hercules will still be flying in the mid-21st century, an operating life-span unmatched in military aviation history.

| Technical details: C-130J | |
|---|---|
| **Cost (in millions of dollars):** | 60 |
| **Size:** | |
| Length | 29,79 m |
| Height | 11,84 m |
| Wingspan | 40,41 m |
| Wing area | 162,12 m² |
| Flap area | 31,77 m² |
| Hold area | 39,50 m² |
| **Weight:** | |
| Empty | 34.278 kg |
| Maximum | 79.380 kg |
| Maximum load | 18.955 kg |
| Internal fuel | 25.816 l |
| External fuel | 10.600 l |
| **Engines:** | 4 Rolls-Royce AE2100D3 turboprops, of 4,591 horsepower each, turning R391 six-bladed propellers. |
| **Performance:** | |
| Ceiling | 9.315 m |
| Maximum speed | 645 km/h |
| Time to reach 6.000 m | 12 minutes |
| Take-off requirement | 1.003 m |
| Landing distance | 427 m |
| Maximum range | 5.250 km with 18 tons of cargo |

# US STRATEGIC
## TRANSPORT AIRCRAFT

▲ One of the most significant strategic capabilities of the C-17, the latest models of which weigh slightly more than seventy tonnes, is its ability to carry a main battle tank in its hold.

The American government's desire to maintain a policy of global intervention has led them to establish an air transport capability without parallel in any other country, with a cargo capacity in excess of that of the largest civilian companies.

The recent conflicts in Afghanistan, Iraq and Kuwait have demonstrated that this capability allows for rapid intervention in any part of the world, independently of the type of troops or materiel which has to be transported. This capability, which is largely the responsibility of the Air Mobility Command (AMC) of the United States Air Force (USAF), is based on several hundred high-volume transport aircraft, which are considered to be strategic due to their performance and potential.

### A long and continuing process

The means employed today were first under consideration forty years ago. The design of the first plane making up the present-day triumvirate, specifically the C-141 Starlifter, was under-

taken at the beginning of the 1960s. This design is now obsolescent, but it has served well and will continue flying for several years. The first milestone in its manufacture by Lockheed, now the Lockheed Martin Corporation, came with the delivery of the first plane, which received the military designation C-141A, in October 1964.

It took three more years to complete the USAF order for what was, in those days, the first high-volume jet-powered transport plane. A major design factor was the need to transport troops and materiel anywhere in the world and, as a result, the plane was designed with a long fuselage and a very large wing. Its performance, which was received with satisfaction by its users, would lead it to play an especially active part in the Vietnam War, where it was used, for example, to evacuate five hundred American prisoners of war freed at the end of hostilities. Another of the landmarks achieved by this plane was that it was the first jet plane used to drop paratroops, and also the first to land in Antarctica. To adapt its performance to future needs, it was decided to design a version with a lengthened fuselage, designated the C-141B, which started to enter service in 1979. This version was followed by the C-141C, which was the result of upgrading the current aircraft to a new standard. This process was completed between 1997 and 2001.

At present, despite the fact that the last version has redesigned avionics and can receive fuel in-flight at the rate of ninety thousand litres in twenty-six minutes, it has been relegated to service with the Reserve squadrons and the Air National Guard (ANG). Although it is soon to be withdrawn, it is hoped to squeeze some more service out of it, to exceed ten million hours of active service.

While this happens, the USAF is also planning on keeping the enormous C-5 Galaxy in service

for a few more years. This is the largest military transport plane in the West, and while planning on this model also started in the 1960s its entry into service was delayed until June 1970, when Lockheed delivered the first C-5A to the 437th Airlift Wing at Charleston Air Force Base.

This plane includes some special features designed to ease military transport requirements. Its nose opens upwards, like an enormous mouth, to give free access to the hold. This makes it easy to load the largest and heaviest of cargo, like tanks, helicopters, containers, and cargo on pallets.

Its capacity enables it to carry objects as big as a seventy-four tonne bridge, or an M-1 Abrams, which weighs nearly sixty tonnes. This capacity was improved with the arrival of the C-5B in the second half of the 1980s. Overall, the USAF received fifty C-5B and seventy-six C-5A. One of the most noteworthy aspects of the Galaxy is that, at full load, it only needs runways of 2,530 metres to take off, and of 1,493 metres to land. The configuration of its landing-gear is also notable, consisting of twenty-eight wheels to support its massive weight. This can reach three hundred and eighty tonnes in war-time: included in this, apart from the weight of the plane itself, is up to one hundred and fifty tonnes of fuel and one hundred and twenty-two tonnes of all types of cargo.

Its pilots appreciate its cargo-loading flexibility and, equally, its ability to operate, occasionally, from semi-prepared airfields. There are eight hundred sensors distributed strategically throughout the aircraft that analyse the workings of all its equipment and warn of any defect. Despite this, the AMP (Avionics Modernization Program) was put in hand in 1998 with the aim of upgrading its equipment, adapting it to current air traffic-control requirements and improving its navigational ability.

Its in-flight refuelling ability increases its already extensive range using a standard fuel load. This is five thousand miles at full load and six thousand three hundred when flying empty. Its price exceeds two hundred million dollars at current prices, which is not a great deal taking into account its operational capability and its characteristic ease of maintenance and efficiency. A recent metal fatigue study carried out on the fuselage

structure found that it still has 80% of its useful life remaining, which says a lot for the technology and materials employed in its construction.

## A new contribution

The planes described above fulfilled USAF requirements which are now obsolete, so it has been necessary to modernise them. In order to satisfy these new requirements, three proposals, competing under the C-X programme, were evaluated as recently as the early 1980s. Finally, the McDonnell Douglas option was chosen on 28th August, 1981. Owing to the normal delays inherent in development, the contract to build three C-17 prototypes was signed four years later,

the first of which was not ready until 21st December, 1990, which shows how strict the initial design and manufacturing process was. A further nine months went by before the trials programme began, with test flights to check the performance of the three available planes. The tests to check compliance with all the preset targets were very strict. The first production aircraft, by now named the Globemaster III, was handed over in May, 1992, almost eleven years after its selection as a candidate. This long drawn out period, unusual for a transport plane, allowed new technology to be incorporated in the design and manufacturing processes, which improved performance and allowed the design to be modified to com-

ply strictly with end-user requirements. The initial satisfaction of the USAF was cut short, when they saw their initial plans to acquire two hundred and ten C-17 aircraft reduced gradually to authorisation for only forty. During the past decade, and the first years of the current one, they were able to get this number increased to the level of current forecasts, which are set at the purchase of one hundred and eighty aircraft. The most recent contract, dated August, 2002, talks about spreading the purchase cost of seventy planes over several years, aiming to reduce costs as much as possible, as they have risen substantially above the initial estimate.

The current manufacturer is Boeing, which

produces them at a rate of roughly fifteen per year. This rate has meant that, by the start of 2004, one hundred and seventeen planes had already been delivered to the USAF and the National Guard, apart from the four leased to the Royal Air Force with an option to buy.

Without further orders, the production line will be active until at least 2008. It is highly likely that a further batch will be ordered when the C-141 is finally withdrawn from service. This reduction in transport capacity, along with the excellent performance

demonstrated so far, will mean that further units will probably be built for the USAF. To date, in the few years that the Globemaster III has been in service, it has already obtained thirty-three records for its abilities, more than any other current transport aircraft.

◀ The C-5 Galaxy has been flying for several decades. Despite modernisation, its maintenance requirements are heavier than for more recent aircraft.

▼ The C-141 has been in service for the last four decades, but it still has life remaining. One of its uses is for dropping paratroops.

◀ One of the best features of the C-5 is its opening nose, which lifts to give access to the hold, a complex technical solution, but one that eases movement of vehicles and personnel.

## Military action

At the moment it is used by the 437th Airlift Wing at McChord and Altus Air Force Bases and at Jackson, which belongs to the ANG. Current forecasts talk about new C-17s being based at McGuire and March, the latter as part of the Air Reserve, although changes to these plans are not ruled out. These bases permit a global operating capability, given that this plane is principally designed as a very long-range strategic transport. Among other actions, it has carried out transport and humanitarian aide missions in the Balkans, apart from having a key role in the recent campaigns in Afghanistan and Iraq. One of many examples of its versatility was a mission carried out in 1998, in which eight C-17s transported a paratroop contingent to central Asia, dropping them after a nineteen hour flight. This para-drop mission, an important milestone in military history, was repeated in 2000 and 2003. The plane's remarkable operational ability is due to its capacity and design, which allow it to operate from lightly prepared runways, with loads of a maximum of seventy-seven tonnes in its large hold, including a tank. It only needs a crew of three to fly and obtain this performance, although, on long-distance flights, two crews normally fly, taking turns at the controls.

Four high performance Pratt & Whitney PW 2040 engines, known by the USAF designation F117-PW-100, are fitted on separate underwing pylons. Their exhaust is reversible in the air and on the ground, which, in the latter case, helps to reduce the distance needed to land if the plane is heavily laden. Their fuel consumption is low and is fed from four tanks inside the wings and the body of the plane, which have a total capacity of one hundred and two thousand litres of JP8 or Jet A-1. This quantity of fuel, along with what can be added by in-flight refuelling, gives it an unlimited range that depends only on the crew's endurance. With a standard fuel load, and depending on payload, its range is calculated at around 8,700 kilometres. An interesting technical detail of this model are the winglets (vertical extensions at the end of the wings), which improve aerodynamic efficiency.

The design of the wings is also worthy of note, being adapted for low level flying, along with the huge rear entrance which facilitates loading and unloading. It can drop a detachment of one hundred and two paratroops and their equipment in flight, or it can drop cargo by parachute using LAPES (Low Altitude Parachute Extraction System) or in CDS (Container Delivery System) containers. It is also able to carry ninety wounded, including thirty-six on beds, in a MEDEVAC (Medical Evacuation) role, and is being fitted with the most advanced avionics and electronic navigation systems currently available, such as GATM (Global Air Traffic Management), and the brand- new Northrop LAIRCM (Large Aircraft Infrared Countermeasures) system for self-defence.

▲ *The C-17 can carry most modern equipment anywhere. Here we see helicopters packed inside its cargo compartment.*

| Technical details: C-17 Globemaster III | |
| --- | --- |
| **Cost (in millions of dollars):** | 236,7 |
| **Size:** | |
| Length | 54,04 m |
| Height | 16,79 m |
| Wing area | 353,03 m² |
| Ailerons area | 11,83 m² |
| Fuselage diameter | 6,86 m² |
| **Weight:** | |
| Empty | 22.016 kg |
| Maximum | 265.352 kg |
| Maximum load | 77.292 kg |
| Internal fuel | 102.624 l |
| **Engines:** | 4 Pratt & Whitney F117-PW-100 turbofans delivering 20,000 kilograms of thrust each. |
| **Performance:** | |
| Ceiling | 13.716 m |
| Cruising speed | 0,74-0,77 Mach |
| Landing speed (fully loaded) | 213 km/h |
| Take-off requirement | 470 m |
| Tactical range | 8.700 km |

# EUROPEAN MARITIME
## PATROL AIRCRAFT

In the first chapter of this book we remarked on the existence of a European consortium which manufactures advanced transport aircraft, some of which can be adapted to carry out maritime patrol missions when fitted with special equipment such as the Spanish FITS system.

The present situation differs considerably from that of several decades ago, when the Soviet threat was clear and Russian naval power – expressed by hundreds of submarines ploughing through the seas – made it necessary to possess various means to try and prevent this activity in wartime.

This requirement, supported by the need to carry out tasks relating to maritime surveillance and rescues at sea, led various European aviation manufacturers to work on aircraft projects specifically designed to carry out these tasks. The French Atlantic/Atlantique family, in service with countries like Germany, Italy, Pakistan and France, and the Nimrod, which is only in service with the UK, stand out among the aircraft produced, due to their ability and the range of tasks they perform.

**A shared effort**

The Atlantic is a twin-engined plane designed to specific requirements. The plans, which resulted from a competition in 1958, aimed to offer a platform which would satisfy the needs of various NATO countries. It was initially designated ALT1, referring to the first version, which combined the interests of the four countries which had announced their intention of buying it: Holland, West Germany, Italy and France.

That version, which is still in service with the last three of the above-mentioned countries, was the result of international collaboration

◀ *The British Nimrod is a plane that has evolved over the years. The current standard model has the same external fuselage shape as the original, but very little else.*

▶ *The FITS system consists of advanced sensors and modern information display equipment. The information received by the former is analysed and presented to the operators to take decisions.*

in which the partners had a percentage share based on the number of planes they were thinking of buying. The French were the first to take steps to improve the performance of the Atlantic in May, 1984, by approving the construction of an improved series of thirty model ALT2 aircraft.

More recently, the management of Dassault Aviation presented the ALT3, a new generation which marries a new body cell with up-to-the-minute mission avionics, as well as more powerful engines and improved performance propellers. No sales have been confirmed, although the Italians, who had decided to replace this plane, in the end decided to upgrade theirs by fitting Thomson CSF Iguane radar, GEC Avionics AQS-902 acoustic systems and other equipment. As for the Germans, they reinforced their planes' body cells and installed modern avionics and sensors, such as a Texas Instruments APS-134(V) radar, together with electronic countermeasure

containers on the trailing edges of the wings. The operators are planning to reduce the number of planes in active service, while maintaining their capabilities, because the Atlantic has a spacious cargo area and is able to carry two and a half tonnes of armament, to negate the threat posed by submarines and surface ships. Currently, they are used for many more tasks, and are as likely to be used trying to locate boats with illegal immigrants on-board, or spotting unauthorised dumping of illegal substances at sea, although the full military potential of their sensors, like the sonar buoys or magnetic anomaly detector, is kept up-to-date.

**British self-sufficiency**

At the same time that the aircraft mentioned above were being built, the Royal Air Force (RAF) took the decision to obtain a new anti-submarine aircraft to replace the types in use until then. From the beginning of the

design process, the first prototype of the new offering from Hawker Siddeley (now British Aerospace) received the designation Nimrod. To cut costs, its development was based on the fuselage of the Comet civil airliner. They were looking for an already proven platform, powered by jet engines, which would, in principle, allow for a higher patrol speed and a more extensive search area.

The RAF contract – for thirty-eight aircraft – began to be fulfilled, strictly speaking, with the flight of the first production aircraft, on 28th June, 1968. Production was completed in less than four years, at which point another eight planes, Mark 1s this time, were ordered to be held as replacements for possible losses.

Modernisation, which included improved avionics and sensors, was delayed, and the first of the definitive version was not ready until 1979, which enabled a total of thirty-five planes to be refitted, including all the new ones and

some of the previous ones. As a result of the differences between the performance of these planes and the initial batch, they were designated Mark 2.

Its capabilities were put to the test during the Falklands conflict of 1982, which resulted in a minor refit: in-flight refuelling probes were installed to increase the patrol radius to nineteen hours, underwing rails for AIM-9 Sidewinder self-defence missiles were fitted and they were even equipped with new electronic countermeasures.

With the passage of time, a further upgrade became necessary, and was ordered in 1996, with completion due in 2009, when the last of the eighteen planes ordered is due to be ready. The new Nimrod, designated MRA4 (Maritime Reconnaissance and Attack Mark 4), is a totally different plane, sharing only the basic fuselage with the original. The cockpit is based on the Airbus family of airliners; the radar is a Racal Searchwater 2000MR, capable of coping with hundreds of contacts; the acoustic suite is the Canadian-designed AQS-970, which includes a Lockheed Martin self-protection sub-system. A Magnetic Anomaly Detector, Northrop Grumman Night Giant search and detection system and a full electronics and communications suite will be fitted, all integrated within a specially developed Tactical Command System (TCS).

This transformation, which will, in theory, cost two thousand million pounds sterling, will enable the planes to carry out effective anti-submarine patrol, anti-surface unit attack and even search and rescue missions. Currently, the Nimrod is the only jet-powered maritime patrol aircraft in service, anywhere in the world.

One of Europe's most recent successes has been the sale of the CN-235 to the United States Coast Guard. These planes will be used to patrol US territorial waters.

## Technical details

| | Atlantic 2 | Nimrod MRA 4 |
|---|---|---|
| **Cost (in millions of dollars):** | 100 | 140 |
| **Size:** | | |
| Length | 33,63 m | 38,63 m |
| Height | 11,30 m | 9,06 m |
| Wingspan | 37,46 m | 38,71 m |
| Wing area | 120,34 m² | 235,00 m² |
| Flap area | 24,42 m² | --- |
| Cabin working area | 155,00 m² | 196,40 m² |
| **Weight:** | | |
| Empty | 25.600 kg | 45.500 kg |
| Maximum | 46.200 kg | 90.000 kg |
| Maximum external load | 3.500 kg | Inside the weapons bay |
| Total war load | 6.000 kg | 6.120 kg |
| Internal fuel | 23.120 l | 48.780 l |
| **Engines:** | 2 Rolls-Royce Tyne RTy.20 Mk.21 turboprops with 6,100 horsepower each | BMW/Rolls-Royce BR710 4 turbofans, with thrust each 6,200 kg |
| **Performance:** | | |
| Ceiling | 9.145 m | 12.800 m |
| Hifh-altitude speed | 648 km/h | 820 km/h |
| Economical speed | 555 km/h | 780 km/h |
| Patrol speed | 315 km/h | 370 km/h |
| Take-off requirement | 1.840 m | 1.400 m |
| Landind distance | 1.500 m | 800 m |
| Operating range | 1.500 km + 5 hours searching on station | 2.000 km + 6 hours searching on station |
| Transfer range | 9.075 km | 10.000 km |

# P-3 ORION,
## CAPABLE AND MULTI-ROLE

A milestone in the history of naval aviation occurred towards the end of 2003. A P-3C Orion maritime patrol aircraft belonging to the United States Navy managed to fly a UAV (Unmanned Aerial Vehicle) by remote control, making it take-off and obtaining information from its sensors in real-time.

This new capability, which will be rolled out to the US P-3C fleet over the next few years, increases the potential of this plane, which has already carried out a multitude of missions over the last forty years, from hunting Soviet submarines in the 1970s and 1980s, to intelligence gathering during the wars in Afghanistan in 2002 and Iraq in 2003.
The data obtained by its sensors were instantly relayed to ground troops, especially US Marine Corps contingents, to enable them to carry out ground operations.

**A clear need**
These capabilities, which have evolved in parallel with anticipated threats and have led to a great increase in operating potential, first saw the light of day towards the end of the fifties – to be precise, in 1958 – when Lockheed won the programme to build an anti-submarine aircraft based on the commercial Electra airliner.

The first prototype flew in August, 1958, followed in November of the following year by the YP-3A, which was already fitted out with the majority of the equipment and avionics needed to carry out the mission for which it had been designed. The results were so satisfactory that the US Navy decided to buy it and signed the contract for full-scale production, with the aircraft entering service in 1962.

A few years later, they decided to buy a version with more powerful turboprop engines, specifically the Allison T-56-A-14, giving rise to the P-3B. It was a great commercial success, with one hundred and twenty-four sold to the US Navy, five to Norway, five more to New Zealand, and ten to Australia. The C version flew before the end of the same decade, fitted with new sensors and equipment linked to a Univac digital computer, which allowed the best use to be made of them.

Its capabilities encouraged the US Navy to buy a further one hundred and forty-three planes between 1969 and 1978, a contract which was completed at the same time as the avionics fitted to the rest were upgraded, first to P-3C Update standard, and then, to Update II. This latter change included an Infrared Detecting Set (IRDS), the fitting of the SRS system, which allows better use to be made of sonar buoys, and the ability to carry and fire the Harpoon anti-ship missile. These changes encouraged the Dutch Navy to place an order for thirteen aircraft.

Development did not stop there, and Update III arrived, an important feature of which is the introduction of a new acoustic processor, specifically the IBM UYS-1 Proteus. Further details were also included, such as greater crew comfort, and the installation of an improved, and more powerful auxiliary unit, a useful

piece of equipment which allows the plane to start-up without outside assistance.

**New capabilities**

The entire modernisation process has been permanently ongoing and carried out almost continuously. In 1991, it was decided to implement Update IV in eighty aircraft, but budget cuts prevented it. What was in fact carried out, as a result of inadequacies noted during the 1991 Gulf War, was an upgrade to P-3C Update III AIP (Anti-surface warfare Improvement Program) standard, which has meant being able to count on new capabilities since 1998. These have meant it being modified to fire the infrared Maverick missile, an air-to-surface weapon that can sink ships at sea or destroy land-based targets. It was also fitted with systems such as the infrared detector IRDS AN/AAS-36A, which can detect chan-

The sonar buoy launcher is situated in the lower part of the P-3's fuselage. These are devices which are dropped on the water so that their sensors can locate anything underwater.

The Orion's cockpit is quite spacious, and the pilots have a good view. Naval patrol missions require fixed manoeuvres to be carried out flying just above wave height.

ges in heat generation with great accuracy; the electro-optical AN/AVX-1 sensor, which is used to obtain video images which are very useful for reconnaissance and surveillance missions; the AN/APS-173B(V) radar, which is a multi-role set, able to detect targets as small as a the periscope of a submarine; and the EP-2060 pulse analyser, which, linked to the AN/ALR-66 system, can detect, process and display electromagnetic emissions from naval, ground or aerial sources.

The upgrade of Orion to the most advanced current level include all of this new generation of equipment as standard, along with an upgrade to the displays for the pilots and crew, as well as a long-range OASIS III (Over the horizon Airborne Sensor Information System) transmitter, which makes it easier to transfer data to other friendly platforms. These improvements were combat-tested in Operation Allied Force, when the North Atlantic Treaty Organisation (NATO) faced Serbian forces over Kosovo in 1999. Flying from the Adriatic Sea, planes upgraded to this standard were very useful supporting the firing of Tomahawk TLAM (Land Attack Missile, Tactical). At the same time, the images obtained by their sensors enabled the position of more than three thousand targets to be identified and transmitted in an instant to the military operation's Command Centre, and they were also very useful in the subsequent phases of the operation, acting against illegal smuggling.

These successes encouraged the US Chief of Naval Operations (CNO) to seek an improvement in the Orion's capabilities, this time to help in the fight against drug-smuggling. This new model, which has acquired the initials CDUE (Counter-Drug Update Equipment), is notable for having AN/APG-66 air-to-air radar and for including sophisticated communications equipment and a modern AN/AVX-1(V) sensor.

## Changing missions

All these technological changes, and the aircraft's capabilities, have not only interested the US Navy, which has bought more than five hundred of them in various configurations, but other countries too, including Spain, Argentina, Canada, Chile, Brazil, Japan, Greece, South Korea, Portugal, and even Iran, which has signed contracts to upgrade its planes to the P-3B FITSS version, although the Iranian planes are only functioning at minimum operative levels. This commercial success is due to the happy combination of a tried and tested platform, with the fitting of equipment adapted precisely to the requirements of the threat, allowing capabilities to be modernised at relatively low cost, and the introduction of new technology that significantly strengthens its role as the airborne pillar of naval control operations. At the same time, traditional maritime patrol missions have also evolved into other, more specialised ones, and the plane's multi-role ability is more compatible with present-day military requirements. It is important to note that the Orion stands out in having an extensive patrol range, with a fuel tank in the fuselage and four more in the two wings. Its power-plant comprises four engines, although it can fly on only two or three, which is a normal procedure used to save fuel and to increase the range flown. It holds the world speed record for a turbo-prop aircraft, reaching 806.10 km/h in a level flight. On maritime patrols, it is normal to fly just above sea-level to increase the chance of locating targets. It also offers significant support to its eleven crew members, three of whom fly the plane with the rest operating the sensors from consoles inside the fuselage. To make long missions easier, there are basic facilities such as a kitchen, fridge and rest area. Finally, in addition to the sensors, it is able to drop various types of sonar buoys, a device with hydrophones designed to locate submarines. It can also set off markers which colour the water or which release smoke to make visual spotting even easier. Its armament, carried in the weapons-bay and on ten underwing pylons, can include torpedoes, mines, depth charges, anti-ship missiles, air-to-air missiles for self-defence, and even Mk.57 nuclear bombs. These are designed to explode underwater and destroy submarines by the pressure wave generated by their 5 or 10 kilotonne warhead.

The costly MMA (Multi-mission Maritime Aircraft) programme has already been launched to replace the omnipresent Orion with an equally capable multi-role aircraft, due to enter service around 2012.

◁ This photograph is of the lower part of a P-3, showing the weapons-bay doors in the open position, and the location of the sonar buoy launcher.

◁ ◁ The offensive capability of the P-3 is clear from this photo, showing one of these planes fitted with four anti-ship missiles, which can hit targets 100 kilometres away.

| Technical details: P-3C Orion | |
|---|---|
| **Cost (in millions of dollars):** | 60 |
| **Size:** | |
| Length | 35,61 m |
| Height | 10,27 m |
| Wingspan | 30,37 m |
| Wing area | 120,77 m² |
| Flap area | 19,32 m² |
| Cabin area | 61,13 m² |
| **Weight:** | |
| Empty | 27.890 kg |
| Maximum | 64.410 kg |
| Maximum weapons load | 9.071 kg |
| Fuel | 34.826 l |
| **Engines** | 4 Allison T56-A-14 turboprops producing 4,910 horsepower each, turning four-bladed Hamilton Standard 54H60-77 fixed-speed |
| **Performance:** | |
| Ceiling | 8.625 m |
| High-altitude speed | 761 km/h |
| Patrol speed | 381 km/h |
| Take-off requirement | 1.290 m |
| Operational range | 2.494 km + 3 hours on station |
| Transit range | 7.670 km |

# S-3 VIKING
## MORE THAN JUST A SUB-CHASER

The S-3 Viking was designed to be the main anti-submarine weapon protecting US Navy aircraft-carriers and their escort ships.

The thirty years of active service it has completed have enabled it to consolidate its ability to carry out its primary role, as well as demonstrating that the plane is sufficiently capable of taking on complementary tasks supporting carrier air-groups.

**Satisfying a need**

It was the mid-1960s when the United States Navy first started to consider the need to design a plane to replace the S-2 Tracker in the carrier-borne anti-submarine warfare (ASW) role. Five proposals were initially considered for the project, which finally resulted in the awarding of a contract worth 462 million dollars to the Lockheed Corporation

to produce the design they had proposed. Lockheed Corporation started the development work, which also involved other companies: Vought were in charge of the wings, the landing-gear and the engine gondolas, while Univac's contribution was the computer charged with processing the information obtained by the various sensors.

The external support given by this association of companies led to the first prototype being completed in a relatively short period of time. The S-3's first flight took place on the 21st January, 1972. A further eight machines followed and these were used to evaluate its performance, analyse its potential and to develop its equipment, with the whole process procee-

ding, most unusually, at a very fast pace.

Only two years later, specifically in February 1974, the first S-3As were delivered to the US Navy. They were allocated to VS-41, a Training Squadron based at North Island Naval Air Station, California. The following year, the first machines were embarked on the aircraft-carrier USS John F.Kennedy, and their entry into operational service was judged very positively. Manufacture of the last of the 187 aircraft ordered took place in mid-1978, and, as a result, the production line at Lockheed's in Burbank was shut down.

From the start of the programme, it had been envisaged that initial performance and the data-processing capacity of the various pie-

▲ The Viking was designed to be based on US aircraft-carriers. A characteristic feature is the folding wings, which reduces the wing-span and hence the space occupied on-board.

◀ One of the most recent tasks the S-3 design has been adapted to carry out has been that of flying tanker, to supply fuel to other naval aircraft.

ces of equipment would be progressively increased, and that new systems would be fitted. The first step in this direction was taken in the early 1980s and was designated the WSIP (Weapons System Improvement Program), a collection of upgrades which improved the operational ability to use various weapons systems, with the aim being to evolve from the initial purely anti-submarine capability into a platform which could also be used to fight other threats, principally surface-based.

## Improved capabilities

As part of this process, the manufacture of the equipment necessary for this transformation was put in hand and, over the course of the decade, it was fitted to the aircraft allocated to the squadrons operating with the Atlantic and Pacific Fleets. In the 1990s, work was carried out to upgrade the Viking to the S-3B version, which involved modernising its processing and

display capacity, fitting an ISAR/SAR synthetic aperture radar that works in conjunction with a new infrared detector, and the modification of the underwing pylons to enable long-range anti-ship missiles, such as the AGM-84 Harpoon, to be carried. The most recent modernisation, which was trialled in tests which took place at the end of March 2003, is the modification of the plane to enable it to attack using laser-guided missiles, specifically the AGM-65 Maverick. This use has so far been restricted to Operation Iraqi Freedom and included an attack on a naval target on the river Tigris, near the Iraqi city of Basra.

This process of evolution, which includes the possibility, in the medium-term, of also being able to launch torpedoes or AGM-84 SLAM-ER (Stand-off Land Attack Missile, Extended Range) ground attack missiles, also foresees a gradual reduction in the number of planes and their use in new types of missions, because

| Technical details: S-3B Viking | |
|---|---|
| **Cost (in millions of dollars):** | 45 |
| **Size:** | |
| Length | 16,26 m |
| Height | 6,93 m |
| Wingspan | 20,93 m |
| Wing area | 55,74 m² |
| **Weight:** | |
| Empty | 10.954 kg |
| Maximum | 23.643 kg |
| Internal fuel | 7.192 l |
| External fuel | 2.272 l |
| **Engines:** | 4 Allison T56-A-14 turboprops producing 4,910 horsepower each, turning four-bladed Hamilton Standard 54H60-77 fixed-speed propellers |
| **Performance:** | |
| Ceiling | 12.200 m |
| Maximum speed | 828,8 km/h |
| Take-off requirement | 807 m |
| Range | 4.232 km |

◀ ◀ *S-3's are moved from the hangar to the carrier's flight deck by the lifts. Its size enables two to be moved at once.*

◀ *The cockpit has large glazed areas, giving the pilots and the rest of the four man crew good all-round vision.*

the number of purely anti-submarine missions has declined dramatically in comparison to the recent past, due to the removal of the Soviet threat.

In view of this, and taking the original airframe as a starting point, variants such as the US-3A have been produced, with all the avionics stripped out, so that the plane can be used as a liaison aircraft or a light transport. The KS-3A is fitted with Sargent Fletcher underwing pods that enable it to refuel other aircraft inflight, acting as a limited capacity tanker. During this transformation process, the ES-3A

Shadow was also designed, converting 16 of the older airframes into highly capable electronic warfare aircraft able to capture and analyse electronic emissions from naval units or ground locations. They were all removed from active service in 1999. It can be said that Viking missions today are limited to acting against hostile targets, aerial refuelling, surveillance, search and rescue, and command and control. However, these can be all-weather, night and day missions, further proof of the plane's worth. It has proved possible to perform these various missions, in addition to the anti-subma-

rine warfare role, because the original design was very adaptable.

The crew consists of two pilots, who fly the plane from a cockpit located at the front of a cabin laid out in the traditional manner, and a further two systems operators in the rear of the cabin. It has an extensive range and its flight envelope is fairly good, due to the use of two very reliable and powerful turbofans, which are both installed in underwing gondolas. Additionally, it has been fitted with the equipment necessary to receive fuel in-flight, to improve its range.

# AERIAL REFUELLING
## TANKERS

In recent decades, air missions have taken place in a variety of situations and locations, often characterised by their distance from air-bases and other support centres. Given that strike planes, helicopters and transports all have a limited range when operating dependant on their own fuel loads, it has been necessary to invent ways to increase this range and to allow aircraft to reach their targets and return without having to abort a mission half way through.

To meet this need, specially modified planes have been designed to supply the others with their precious fuel whilst airborne. In general terms, they are known as aerial refuelling tankers and the extent of the problem has meant that increasing numbers of air forces have taken to using them in order to be self-sufficient in this respect.

**A historical overview**

The first airborne refuelling operations took place in 1923, the protagonists being DH-4 biplanes. Since then, many things have changed, with great advances taking place in this field. Multi-role aircraft have emerged

to carry out this task, as well as other, more specialised roles, which have been designed for it exclusively.

The usefulness of this role was amply demonstrated in the coalition attacks on Iraq in 2003, as it had been in previous air campaigns. During the Falklands War in 1982, British Vulcan bombers flew six bombing missions from Ascension Island, which were the longest combat flights in history at the time, each raid of two aircraft requiring eleven flights by Victor tankers to refuel the bombers and the tankers themselves, in a complicated relay operation. In 1981, the Israelis had used the same technique when

carrying out their daring attack on the Iraqi nuclear facility at Osirak, which was prevented from ever entering service by the accuracy of the bombs dropped by their F-16s. The annual Spanish deployment of their F-18 Hornet aircraft to Nellis Air Force Base in Nevada for advanced tactical training is a more conventional example of a mission requiring air-to-air refuelling, with careful planning of each of the refuelling missions necessary to allow the fighters to reach a destination so far away.

These concrete examples are the result of standardised procedures and a methodology in training different pilots, irrespective of

the type of plane they fly. Training is even more intense for those who have a special aptitude for it or who are going to need to use it under extreme conditions. Additionally, this training ensures that missions are longer and that the load carried – weapons or cargo, depending on the type of aircraft – is greater, because it is possible to readjust with the limits on maximum take-off weight.

At an operational level, detailed planning of the sequence of events and of the location of the rendezvous between the tanker and the plane which needs fuel is carried out. To ensure this rendezvous is met, measures such as global positioning by satellite and radio encryption equipment are used.

### Working philosophy

The receiving aircraft must be fitted with the necessary equipment to allow it to receive fuel. This can be a fixed probe, which is the most common, a retractable probe, which is extended mechanically at the appropriate time, or a receiver, normally located on the upper part of the

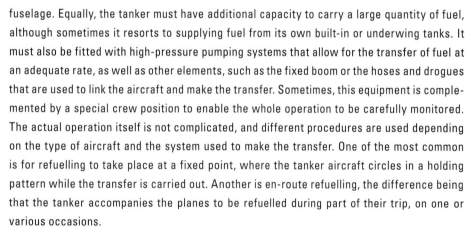

fuselage. Equally, the tanker must have additional capacity to carry a large quantity of fuel, although sometimes it resorts to supplying fuel from its own built-in or underwing tanks. It must also be fitted with high-pressure pumping systems that allow for the transfer of fuel at an adequate rate, as well as other elements, such as the fixed boom or the hoses and drogues that are used to link the aircraft and make the transfer. Sometimes, this equipment is complemented by a special crew position to enable the whole operation to be carefully monitored. The actual operation itself is not complicated, and different procedures are used depending on the type of aircraft and the system used to make the transfer. One of the most common is for refuelling to take place at a fixed point, where the tanker aircraft circles in a holding pattern while the transfer is carried out. Another is en-route refuelling, the difference being that the tanker accompanies the planes to be refuelled during part of their trip, on one or various occasions.

Less frequent is circuit refuelling, which is used when the weather conditions are bad or for emergency refuelling. In this case, it is the tanker aircraft which makes its way to meet the receiving aircraft, to help it out by topping up its fuel.

These three methods require prior establishment of an Air Refuelling Control Point (ARCP) and an Air Refuelling Control Time (ARCT) to enable the rendezvous to take place. Similarly, alternatives are agreed, in case it proves impossible to make the main one. In the pre-flight planning phase, aspects such as speed, altitude, fuel quantity and elements affecting navigation, among others, are analysed.

**The different planes**

Operators use planes which have been specially modified for this role. The British have the British Aerospace VC10 K.Mk.2/3 and the Lockheed L-1011-500 Tristar, both originally commercial airliners which will be replaced by the new Airbus A330-200, recently chosen to fulfil the MRTT (Multi-Role Tanker Transport) requirement. The Spanish use the KC-130H

(based on the Hercules transport), specially modified with tanks which can be assembled inside the cargo-bay and fitted under the wing. The Russians use the Iluyshin Il-78 Midas, a modified strategic transport plane, and the Tupolev Tu-16N, based on the Badger bomber, while countries such as Australia, Canada and Israel use different modifications of the basic Boeing 707 platform.

The largest fleet of aerial refuelling tankers is used by the United States, given the size of its budgetary resources and requirements for strategic deployments. To illustrate the latter, consider a statistic from the 1991 Gulf War campaign, when roughly 26,000 such movements were made, a similar figure to the campaigns in Afghanistan in 2002, and Iraq in 2003. So many hours were flown that those in charge of the United States Air Force have been obliged to consider ordering a new tanker aircraft to mitigate the effects of the high number of flying hours accumulated by the planes currently in service.

The aircraft chosen was the KC-767, a modified Boeing 767 airliner already in service with Japan and Italy. A preliminary agreement has been signed with the company, opting for a long-term leasing arrangement which will enable one hundred of these planes to enter service. However, recent negative reports from the Pentagon give reason to believe that this decision may be changed.

Meanwhile, they continue to rely on more than five hundred KC-135 Stratotankers and

*The KC-10 has a standard supply pole (boom), located aft in the lower part of the fuselage. The small wings fitted to the pole are to stabilise it and to guide it to the receiving aircraft.*

*Close-up of the control position from which the fuel transfer operation is monitored on board a USAF tanker. It is vital that the manoeuvre is carried out within the established guidelines.*

fifty KC-10 Extender tankers. The former have been flying since 1954 and are also in service with France, Turkey and Singapore. They saw the light of day at the same time as the Boeing 707 airliner, whose design they share. Their original four jet engines were replaced by more efficient, quieter CFM-56 turbines in the majority of the fleet, planes so equipped being designated KC-135R or KC-135T Also in active service is the KC-135E, fitted with TF-33-PW-102 engines.

Changing the original power plant in all of these planes led to an increase in the fuel load carried and a reduction in fuel consumption and operating costs. Basically, they can cover a distance of roughly two thousand five hundred kilometres carrying a fuel load of sixty-eight tonnes in their internal tanks, using an extendable probe called a Boom to transfer this to the receiving aircraft. Around fifty have been fitted with the Mark 32B hose and drogue equipment, enabling them to refuel US Navy planes and those belonging to other NATO allies.

The three-engined KC-10 is both bigger and more capable and is based on the widely-used McDonnell Douglas DC-10 airliner (now the Boeing MD-10). It entered service in 1981 and, since then, it has been extremely active as its transfer rate is better – it can carry 160.200 tonnes of fuel, and transfer it, normally using the extendable boom, at a rate of 4,180 litres per minute. On rare occasions, because the transfer rate is only a third of this, it can resort to using underwing containers and the drogue. The USAF anticipates starting to retire the Stratotanker in 2010, although some of the KC-135R might continue flying till 2030 and beyond if certain equipment is modernised. The Extender has a longer residual service life, although this could be drastically reduced if the demands of the first years of the 21st century are maintained. For this reason, the arrival of a new aircraft is essential, both from a tactical and a technical point of view.

▲ This technique allows the range or duration of a mission to be increased. Electronic monitoring aircraft are also refuelled in flight.

| Technical details | KC-135 | KC-10 |
|---|---|---|
| **Cost (in millions of dollars):** | 50 | 88,4 |
| **Size:** | | |
| Length | 41,53 m | 54,40 m |
| Height | 12,70 m | 17,40 m |
| Wingspan | 39,88 m | 50,00 m |
| **Weight:** | | |
| Empty | 44.464 kg | 105.300 kg |
| Maximum | 146.285 kg | 265.500 kg |
| Maximum fuel load | 90.716 kg | 160.200 kg |
| **Performance:** | | |
| Ceiling | 15.240 m | 12.727 m |
| Maximum speed | 940 km/h | 964 km/h |
| Take-off requirement | 1.200 m | 1.200 m |
| Operating range | 2.419 km | 7.000 km |

# THE C-101 AVIOJET
## SPANISH LIGHT JET

The air forces of Spain, Jordan, Honduras and Chile all use the Aviojet for pilot training or for light tactical support missions. This is a second-generation basic trainer, which combines useful abilities with performance appropriate to its low operating and acquisition costs.

## The project

The development of the C-101 started in the summer of 1974, and was carried out by engineers from the Spanish Construcciones Aeronáuticas S.A. (CASA), now part of EADS/CASA. Their aim was to design a jet which could be used for fighter pilots' basic and advanced training over the next two decades.

The design stage was extremely short, thanks to the help of Germany's MBB and the US company, Northrop. The first prototype was presented to the public on 27th May, 1977 and first flew the following month. In 1978, having carefully evaluated the four pre-production examples, the Spanish Air Force (Ejército del Aire) ordered 60 of the EB model, which were delivered

between October, 1979 and the end of 1982. Their destination was the General Air Academy at San Javier in Murcia province, southeast Spain, and they are used by the instructors of the school as part of the Aguila (Eagle) Aerobatic Display team, although some have also been used temporarily on tactical missions or in exercises as the attacking force. Their number was later increased by 28 additional planes that were assigned to the Schools Group based at Matacán in Salamanca province in western Spain. Their Spanish designation is the E.25 Mirlo. The Spanish experience helped to persuade other users. The first country to order them was Chile, which received around thirty planes from 1981 on, although a fair proportion of them were jointly manufactured and assembled locally by ENAER. They use the CC version, which is designated Halcón (Falcon), although they also use the BB version.

Further orders arrived later: four for Honduras, with different avionics, and sixteen of the CC version for the Jordanian Air Force, the latter being delivered between 1987 and 1988. Current plans for the Aviojets in service with the Spanish Air Force intend keeping them in service for a decade or more, when they will be replaced by the Eurotrainer, which is currently at the project stage. This extension of their service life will require some changes, above all in the lay-out of the cockpit displays which will incorporate recent technical developments by adopting a digital format.

**Varied capabilities**

Taking the standard model as the base, a more capable ground-attack version, the BB, was designed, and was bought by Chile and Honduras. It includes a more powerful engine and other minor modifications.

The CC is an even more sophisticated version. This includes equipment such as a radar detector and a Heads Up Display (HUD) – initially a GEC Ferranti FD4513 –, a weapons control system and more modern communications, as well as an increase in the number of weapon fixing-points that allow it to carry more than two tonnes of bombs, rockets and missiles.

The possibility of using it as an alternative, if limited, combat plane and the expectation of possible sales of such a version, led to the

*Sales of the C-101 to several countries have given it a certain momentum internationally, despite its performance being somewhat lower than its competitors - but then, its price is too!*

design of a more powerful variant designated DD, the prototype flying for the first time on 20th May 1985. It was fitted with a jet engine that generates 2,132 kg of thrust and an integrated navigation and attack system. This version was intended to be used for training in flight techniques and weapon management trials before progressing on to modern combat aircraft. It included improvements such as mission processors, an inertial platform and a display and control unit, all linked with a 1553B data bus.

Nevertheless, the greatest success of the Aviojet has been as a flight trainer, with slightly more than one hundred being constructed. The design concept for this role is quite interesting, above all the modular fuselage design that allows it to withstand the high aerodynamic loads generated by harsh conditions during training and ground

attack missions. It has a useful life estimated at ten thousand flying hours and limiting factors which enable it to range from +7.7 to -3.9 G.

The design includes a twin cockpit with great visibility, with the seats being sited in tandem. The pupil sits in the forward seat with the instructor behind, both seats being Martin-Baker Mk.10 ejector seats. Another interesting feature is the wing, manufactured as one piece and boasting good aerodynamic efficiency and structural rigidity, increased manoeuvrability and more space for the built-in fuel tanks. It is also the only light jet trainer in service to incorporate a weapons bay in the fuselage.

Total fuel capacity is 2,414 litres of JP-4 fuel, although it is normally filled to a maximum of 2,337 litres. This quantity of fuel, allied to the low consumption of its single

Garrett TFE-731-2-2J jet engine generating 1,678 kg of thrust, gives it a large radius of action. It can perform two training missions lasting one hour and ten minutes each, without needing to refuel.

At the same time, as it does not have an afterburner, this aircraft has low noise levels, reduced maintenance costs and low infrared emissions, and incorporates a processor which monitors the engine to ensure that the manufacturer's guidelines are not exceeded in service. It suffers from a certain lack of power, which users have commented on. All the same, the engine enables it to take off in only 13 seconds and in less than 560 metres.

Overall, the C-101 is a capable and cheap training aircraft, which, as long as the cockpit is modernised, could remain in service for many more years.

*The agility of this small Spanish jet has been confirmed at many international air-shows. The risky manoeuvres carried out by the pilots of the Águila aerobatic team always attract attention.*

| Technical details: C-101 DD | |
|---|---|
| Cost (in millions of dollars): | 7 |
| **Size:** | |
| Length | 12,50 m |
| Height | 4,25 m |
| Wingspan | 10,60 m |
| Wing area | 20,00 m² |
| Flap area | 2,50 m² |
| **Weight:** | |
| Empty | 3.470 kg |
| Maximum | 6.300 kg |
| Maximum external load | 2.250 kg |
| Internal fuel | 2.414 l |
| **Engines:** | One Garrett TFE-731-5with 2,132 kg of thrust |
| **Performance:** | |
| Ceiling | 13.410 m |
| Maximum speed | 0,8 Mach |
| Take-off requirement | 560 m |
| Combat range | 600 km with a 30mm cannon and two "Maverick" |
| Maximum range | 3.706 km |
| Design load factor | +7,5 g's |

# THE HAWK
## A BRITISH SUCCESS-STORY

The British Aerospace (BAe) Hawk is an advanced trainer chosen by nineteen users worldwide who have ordered nearly nine hundred planes between them.

Its capabilities make it ideal for use as a trainer, as well as conferring it with many options when configured as a light-attack plane. This has been confirmed by more than a million flying hours since 1976, the year in which the Royal Air Force received the first operational aircraft.

### More than just a trainer

The design of this plane dates back to the first months of the 1970s, and a British requirement for one hundred and seventy-six advanced jet trainers.The first order took shape in the form of a contract dated March 1972 and the new Mk1 aircraft began to be delivered four years later, specifically to RAF Valley in Anglesey. Shortly afterwards, it entered service with the Red Arrows, the famous British aerobatic team, who have taken this plane to the limits of its performance in the field of aerobatics.

The UK, which has always known how to maintain special commercial relationships within its spheres of interest, managed to obtain contracts from countries all over the world, especially in Asia and the Middle East. The list of users includes countries such as Saudi Arabia, Australia, Bahrain, Canada, South Korea, Finland, Indonesia, Kenya, Oman, South Africa and Switzerland. To this list can be added India's recent commitment to purchase sixty-six aircraft, forty-two of which will be locally manufactured by Hindustan Aeronautics Limited (HAL) between 2005 and 2010. At the same time, it has also been chosen by the North Atlantic Treaty Organisation (NATO) for use at a Canadian facility where some of the Alliance's fighter pilots are trained.

The T-45A Goshawk is an interesting case, as it is a modification of the British plane to satisfy American requirements for a trainer. Manufactured locally, it is used both by the US Navy and the Marine Corps.

The development of the Hawk has been progressive and successful from a technological and industrial point of view.

The first version supplied to the RAF was the Mk.1, which has been followed by others, such as the Mk.1A, which was adapted for close air-support missions with underwing pylons for AIM-9 Sidewinder missiles, and the 50, 60, 100 – the most recent successful version, and 200 series. The 200 is a single-seater able to carry out close-support 17 missions and which has a substantial combat capability.

This model development has been accompanied by the introduction of new versions of the single jet engine which powers the plane, changes which have increased its power and range. At the same time, the initial weapons load has also been increased to two tonnes on four underwing pylons in the standard two-seater version. There have also been one or two aesthetic and aerodynamic chan-

ges to improve the Hawks' typical flight envelope.

**Interesting features**

The most important contributions made are the changes to the display equipment in the two-seater cockpit. The systems are now digital and include the latest generation multi-function screens, normally referred to as a 'glass cockpit'. This change-over has been applied simultaneously with the development of more capable variants. For example, the 100 series has been developed since 1982, incorporating an engine with 2,630 kg of thrust and even a HOTAS (Hands On Throttle And Stick) flight control system. A laser illuminator and infrared detector were fitted at the front of the plane, while

its offensive capability was increased by being able to carry more than three tonnes of weapons.

A single-seater variant which flew four years later was developed from this basic model. Its most important feature was that it was a multi-role aircraft, able to carry out photographic reconnaissance, battlefield interception, ground-attack and anti-ship patrol missions. This range of service options even required the installation of advanced radar, a piece of equipment which is not usual in this type of training aircraft.

The variant developed by the United States has gone a further step forward. The Goshawk, as it is known locally, has been manufactured by McDonnell Douglas, now Boeing, since the middle of the last decade.

The contract for their manufacture provided for one hundred and eighty seven aircraft incorporating various changes, one of which was replacement of the engines with a Rolls-Royce F405-RR-401 turbofan.

All the versions described above are characterised by being highly manoeuvrable and are able to perform complex aerobatics. This helps make them more effective in pilot training or in carrying out limited combat missions, especially the latest versions. The Hawk is also the only light jet training aircraft capable of supersonic speeds, but only in a dive.

The Hawks layout is similar to other aircraft of its type, with a two-seater cabin which boasts excellent visibility that enables the pilot and instructor to observe everything

going on around them. The canopy is made of an acrylic material that is both transparent and very strong, given that it can stand up to the impact of a one kilogramme bird while travelling at 978 km/h. In case of accidents or emergencies, the Hawk is fitted with Martin-Baker Mk.10LH rocket-assisted ejector seats linked to a detonating cable integrated in the canopy, which is activated milliseconds before ejecting in order to destroy it and thereby avoid wounding the pilot during the ejection process.

**Contrasting capabilities**

The fact that the most recent British order, corresponding to the Hawk 128 model, will enter service in 2008, replacing models such as the Hawk T1, speaks volumes for the future of this aircraft. It is expected to be in service for another twenty-five years and will be used to train the pilots of next generation fighters, such as the Typhoon and the JSF (Joint Strike Fighter). All the aircraft are powered by a Rolls-Royce Adour turbofan, which lacks afterburner, but

features good acceleration and reasonable fuel consumption. The modern versions are somewhat more powerful than their predecessors. This engine is fed by two small air-intakes situated alongside the cockpit and is assisted by a Microturbo turbine to generate the energy necessary to start it.

To give it a useful range, the plane has an 832 litre tank installed in the fuselage, and a 823 litre tank in the wings, to which can be added auxiliary tanks attached to the inner underwing pylons. Some versions also have in-flight refuelling probes that increase their operating range and can also be used on training exercises simulating aerial refuelling. As to equipment, this varies conside-

rably between versions and between the planes used by different countries. Those used by the RAF include a gyroscope, UHF and VHF communications equipment and even an IFF (Identifier Friend or Foe). A modernisation programme has recently been approved which will result in them being fitted with IN/GPS (Inertial Navigation/ Global Positioning System) and even night-flying capability.

The attack versions are slightly more sophisticated as far as systems are concerned: radar detector, HUD information display, impact evaluation system and equipment like the SMS (Stores Management System), which manages the armament carried on each mission.

With respect to the weaponry carried, it is interesting that the different versions modified for attack missions have between three and five fixing points, one of them in the centre of the fuselage. As mentioned previously, the maximum load is between two and three tonnes, although it is more usual to use lower weight configurations to maintain adequate range. Depending on user requirements, the planes can be equipped with rocket-launchers, medium-sized bombs, submunitions dispensers, and even air-to-ground missiles like the AGM-65 Maverick, although future versions are also planned which will use smart weapons that will be both highly accurate and less expensive.

This photo shows the Hawk Mk.1, the version that equips various Royal Air Force squadrons. The planes bought thirty years ago have been followed by more recent purchases.

The Red Arrows are the United Kingdom's aerobatic display team. They are internationally famous for the formations and acrobatics which are a feature of their aerial displays. Their 'mount' is the Hawk.

| Technical details: Hawk 100 series | |
|---|---|
| **Cost (in millions of dollars):** | 19,3 |
| **Size:** | |
| length | 11,68 m |
| Height | 4,16 m |
| Wingspan | 9,84 m |
| Wing area | 16,69 m² |
| Flap area | 2,50 m² |
| **Weight:** | |
| Empty | 4.400 kg |
| Maximum | 9.100 kg |
| Maximum external load | 3.265 kg |
| Internal fuel | 1.655 l |
| External fuel | 1.182 l |
| **Engines:** | One Rolls-Royce Adour Mk.781 turbofan with 2,630 kg of thrust |
| **Performance:** | |
| Ceiling | 13.546 m |
| High-altitude speed | Mach 1,2 |
| Take-off requirement | 640 m |
| Landing distance | 605 m |
| Transfer range | 2.594 km |
| Design load factor | +8 / -4 g's |

# THE FRANCO-GERMAN
## ALPHA JET

The need for an advanced training aircraft to cover the basic training stage of the pilots who were supposed to face a hypothetical invasion from Eastern Europe led to co-operation between several European defence industries and the signing of an agreement between French and German companies for its design.

This plane, called the Alpha Jet, has given rise to a family of jet trainers with a secondary ground-attack role. The Argentinean FMA IA-63 Pampa and the Polish Pzl-Mielec I-22 Iryda M-93 are also descendants of the original design.

**Advanced trainer**

The 1969 Le Bourget air show was the showcase where the first mock-ups of the German company Dornier's P-375 trainer design and the French group Dassault-Bréguet's Br.126 project were presented. After studying the two proposals, as well as the E-650 Eurotrainer proposed by Nord/SNIAS and MBB, on 23rd July, 1970, the French and German governments decided

to proceed with the manufacture of the Alpha Jet, which merged the efforts of the first two companies. On the insistence of the German Luftwaffe, it was decided that the aircraft should be multi-role, with a secondary ability to act as a light-attack jet. The decision to buy four hundred aircraft, two hundred for each country, was ratified on 16th February, 1972, and the first prototype flew in October of the following year. On 13th September, 1973, Belgium announced its intention to buy 33 planes.

Maximum production of thirteen a month was not reached until 1979, partly because different components were manufactured by Dornier, Dassault-Bréguet and the Belgian company

SABCA. More elaborate versions have been developed, based on the initial design, including the MS2 variant exported to Cameroon and Egypt, and the NGEA (Nouvelle Génération École/Appui - New Generation trainer/attack) version which is capable of operating air-to-air and air-to-ground missiles. Most recent of all is the Alpha Jet 3, of which only one prototype has been built and which features multi-function displays and an infrared tracking system, among other upgrades.

The final phase in its development will be the ATS (Advanced Training System) model, which will include equipment identical to that fitted in the Rafale fighter-bomber. Although there have

▶ *This photo taken in the 1970's shows the French production line of this light jet training aircraft.*

◀ *The French have tried to promote the Alpha Jet in those countries which remain in their commercial sphere of influence. The hoped-for success has not materialised, despite some sales.*

so far been no sales of these advanced versions, the Alpha Jet can be judged to have made a positive impact on the world market, as it has been exported to Ivory Coast, Morocco, Nigeria, Qatar and Togo. Germany ceded forty planes to Portugal in exchange for pilot training facilities in Portuguese airspace and the remaining German planes have been phased out or sold.

## Notable performance

The need to use the plane in combat, as well as for training missions, led to design criteria being applied at its conception which give it superior performance to other planes of its type.

For this reason, the power-plant comprises two SNECMA-Turbomeca twin-shaft Larzac 04-C6 turbofans, with turbines fitted with a computer-assisted hydromechanical control system that enable a total of 2,700 kg of thrust to be obtained. This remarkable power enables it to reach a speed approaching Mach 1 in a dive and gives it great agility in engagements and out-flanking manoeuvres. Having two engines means improved safety in the case of possible failures, as well as enabling the pilots to simulate the full range of incidents which can occur in their jet acclimatisation courses.

Both engines are fed by a double air-intake situated very low down on both sides of the fuselage. It has a system which prevents the

formation of ice and allows an intake of up to 28 kilograms of air per second, which adds to the plane's performance.

For example, it can climb at the rate of 3,360 metres per minute, one of the best performances in its class.

The plane is also possesses great operational flexibility, enabling it to cover all stages in a military pilot's training. Other important details are the tandem seating arrangements, with a transparent canopy with great visibility, flight controls which allow both simple and safe flying, and the provision of a very robust undercarriage that enables it to use unprepared runways.

The ex-German planes, which can be identified visually by their sharper, more pointed noses, are fitted with more advanced avionics to allow them to be used in combat support missions. In this role, they are manned by a single pilot, who sits in the forward seat in the cabin, using a HUD-style visor to aim the weapons. The pilot also benefits from equipment such as an Elettronica ELT/156 radar warning receiver, a Lear Siegler LSI 6000E course and altitude reckoning system and a Doppler inertial navigator. Turning to the French aircraft, which, among other differences, lack the arrester gear fitted to the German planes, they are equipped with a TACAN (TACtical Air Navigation) AN/ARN-52 navigator, a Thomson CSF-902 rangefinder, and a VOR/ILS receiver system. Since 1981, the French aerobatic display team, Patrouille de France, has used eight Alpha Jets in their airborne displays.

These systems enable the plane to be employed in close support actions, for which the central pylon would be used to attach a pod containing a Mauser Bk-27 27mm cannon with a high rate of fire. Two pylons under each of the wings enable a total of 2.5 tonnes of weapons to be carried, which range from cluster bombs to anti-ship missiles like the Exocet, which is the option chosen by the Egyptians.

Some versions even allow for the fitting of 310 litre auxiliary fuel tanks, a feature which substantially increases the range, above all for transit or area surveillance missions. It is anticipated that the plane will remain in service into the next decade, although, compared to the initial purchases, the number of planes still in service is low. However, the plane that is supposed to replace it has still not entered the design phase.

▼ *It is quite usual for this type of jet aircraft to fly in pairs, because this permits both individual training and the carrying out of more or less complicated formation manoeuvres.*

| Technical details: Alpha Jet | |
| --- | --- |
| **Cost (in millions of dollars):** | 12 |
| **Size:** | |
| Length | 13,23 m |
| Height | 4,19 m |
| Wingspan | 9,11 m |
| Wing area | 17,50 m² |
| **Weight:** | |
| Empty | 3.515 kg |
| Maximum | 8.000 kg |
| Maximum external load | 2.500 kg |
| Internal fuel | 2.030 l |
| **Engines:** | Two SNECMA/Turbomeca Larzac 04-C6 turbofans without afterburners, generating 1,350 kg thrust each |
| **Performance:** | |
| Ceiling | 14.630 m |
| Maximum speed | 917 km/h |
| Take-off requirement | 370 m |
| Maximum range | 4.000 km |
| Design load factor | +12 / -6,4 g's |

# JET
## TRAINERS

Training future combat pilots requires increasingly modern and capable aircraft which will allow them to adapt to the conditions they will face on their combat missions and deployments. As a result, there has lately been a widespread renewal of the different types of light jet used for this task, with new models coming on to the market in order to satisfy the growing demand for modern training aircraft.

The planes currently on offer fall into two general categories: those resulting from upgrading older versions and those which represent a new generation. These planes also cover a complementary need relating to their potential use in combat missions.

### An Italian success

The commercial success of the MB-326 training plane (which was built from the start of the 1960s until the mid-1970s, with more than eight hundred serving the air forces of Argentina, Australia, Brazil, Ghana, Italy, Paraguay, South Africa, Togo, Tunisia, Zaire and Zambia) encouraged the Italian company, Aeromacchi, to work on a modernised twin-seater capable of satisfying more complex requirements.

Its successor, whose delivery started in 1979, was designated the MB-339, a plane with brilliant performance, which was used by the Argentineans in the 1982 Falklands War, only one year after they began to receive them. This aircraft was sold to several countries and a single-seater was developed for the light attack role, the MB-339C. The CD version, ordered by Italy, New Zealand and Eritrea, was based on this variant, as well as the advanced FD, which has the latest-generation digital display equipment. Since 1982, the Italian national aerobatic display team, Frecce Tricolori, have used ten MB-339A aircraft in their displays.

This commercial success encouraged the heads of Aeromacchi SpA to work on a new project, even more ambitious than the preceding ones. They were initially able to count on the support of the Russian company Yakovlev for help with this new development. This new product, known as the M-346, made its first flight at the end of 2003, and the first deliveries are scheduled for 2007, although at the moment there are no firm orders approved to back it up.

Apart from the Italian air force, a long-standing Aeromacchi customer, sales could be obtained in South America or the Middle East, although the world market is difficult and very competitive. The plane's own characteristics make a good sales pitch: twin-engined, powered by F124-GA-100 turbofans; twin-seater, with both training and attack capabilities; avionics based on digital architecture; HOTAS (Hands On Throttle And Stick) flight control, and a cockpit adapted for night-flying.

### The Russian bid

While sales of the above aircraft are being firmed up, Yakovlev's Russian engineers are

not losing the momentum gained by their joint work with the Italians, and although their product might differ in equipment, it does not as far as exterior aesthetics are concerned. Their offering, known as the Yak-130 is characterised by a design lay-out in which the wing has a notable surface area, and the air intakes are positioned low down, giving it very favourable aerodynamics in all flight envelopes.

Maximum speed is close to 1,000 km/h as a result of the thrust provided by two AI-222-25 engines and the light weight of the aircraft itself, which is a maximum of 6,200 kilograms at take-off. This performance, among other things, was responsible for it being chosen to equip Russia's training squadrons in 2002.

It entered service during 2005, once the acceptance and trials programme has been completed.

Its performance is on a par with that of most modern fighter-bombers, being able to reach an angle of attack of 42° whilst maintaining total control, and being able to carry out manoeuvres involving up to +8 G. To ease pilot transition to more advanced models, it incorporates a modern flight control system and a very up-to-date layout. If necessary, it can act as a close support aircraft, armed with nearly three tonnes of missiles, bombs, and other air-to-air or air-to-ground weapons.

Another Russian proposal is the MiG-AT, a training aircraft developed in the early 1980s in response to Soviet Air Force specifications, although it appears that it was not finally selected. It is configured as a twin-engined aircraft, available with two different power-plants, the Soyuz Rd-1700 and the SNECMA Larzac 04-R20, the latter option coming about as a result of an agreement

demonstrator. Special effort has also been made to incorporate stealth technology in its design and in the choice of materials used in its construction. As a result, at a distance of forty-four kilometres, it presents a radar cross-section of only one square meter. These features, as well as the provision of a radar installation, mean that it is firmly positioned as a light attack aircraft, being able to carry a maximum payload of 4.5 tonnes. Its development, which is already of interest to countries like France and Spain, could lead to a single standard aircraft in service with a good number of European countries. The definition phase is supposed to be completed during 2005, with the first flight taking place in 2009, meaning that its future is still uncertain.

The T-50 Golden Eagle, developed by the South Koreans with the help of the US Lockheed Martin Corporation, is slightly further advanced. This proposal, which has an attack version designated LIFT, has received a first order for twenty-five planes, which will be delivered before the end of this decade.

Currently, its builders are planning on trying to obtain further orders, looking for customers among the present operators of the T-38 Talon, a two-seater training plane which has been in service since the early seventies. The prospects in this market will be difficult, especially if users decide to modernise to the T-38C standard, which the US Air Force has opted to do, enabling them to continue flying until 2020. This change affects the entire cockpit – now totally digital – and the powerplant, and also requires slight modification of the air-intakes situated on either side, in front of its small wings.

All these aircraft, and other less representative planes, will set the standard in the field of jet trainers, aircraft which are indispensable in providing the training for future generations of combat pilots.

signed with the French in September, 1992. The plane is slightly more than ten metres long and its maximum take-off weight is around seven tonnes. It can carry a maximum weapons load of two tonnes, attached to underwing pylons and under the fuselage. One of its main features is that the design opts for a low wing position with two air intakes on the flanks, somewhat backward compared to other designs. Despite this, it can reach a maximum speed of 850 km/h and enjoys remarkable manoeuvrability, which has been demonstrated in the many international air fairs where it has been present.

## Looking to the future

The appearance of new types of jet light trainers is driven by the need to renew some of the planes that have been in service for several decades or to adopt new operating concepts and cheaper maintenance. The MAKO, a plane which is being developed by the European company EADS, working on initial requirements from Germany and the United Arab Emirates, incorporates some of these virtues.

The result of this effort, which involves many companies from different countries, is a compact, fairly squat aircraft. The canopy covering the cockpit differs from previous designs, opening fore and aft rather than to one side. It is powered by a single turbofan, a GE414M that is a variant of the engine used in the F-18 Hornet, in order to save costs and offer increased power.

Another aspect to bear in mind is the quadruple digital flight control system, derived from the one used by the experimental X-31

◀ The MB-339 is an Italian product which has met with success in various markets due to its performance, range and price. The plane currently on offer is descended from this classic.

▲ Aeromacchi MB-339CD is the standard equipment of the training wings of Italy and New Zealand. Its performance is better than other planes of its type.

| Technical details: MB-339FD | |
|---|---|
| Cost (in millions of dollars): | 10 |
| **Size:** | |
| Length | 11,24 m |
| Height | 3,90 m |
| Wingspan | 11,22 m |
| Wing area | 19,30 m² |
| Flap area | 2,21 m² |
| **Weight:** | |
| Empty | 3.414 kg |
| Maximum | 6.350 kg |
| Maximum external load | 1.815 kg |
| Internal fuel | 1.871 l |
| External fuel | 660 l |
| **Engines:** | One Rolls-Royce Viper 680 turbojet with 1,996 kg of thrust |
| **Performance:** | |
| Ceiling | 14.020 m |
| Maximum speed | 920 km/h or 0,8 Mach |
| Take-off requirement | 550 m |
| Maximum range | 2.038 km |
| Design load factor | +7,33 / -4 g's |

# AEW
## FLYING RADAR

◀ The most recent development in the field of airborne early warning systems is Boeing's design for the Australian government.

▶ The Wedgetail, as the new Australian AEW programme is known, is noteworthy for having fixed antenna equipment on the top of the fuselage and not a rotating one as in previous designs.

The acronym AEW (Airborne Early Warning) refers to an aircraft which is fitted with equipment to detect other aircraft in flight over a more or less wide area. The system is usually based on rotating radar or a flat antenna.

These designs, which can only be afforded by the richer nations, are based on sophisticated radars which detect any contact within their operating range.

They transmit pulses which, when they strike an object, be it an actual aircraft or a missile

in flight, are bounced back and received by the same antenna, enabling the object to be positioned on a screen and the operator to know where it is. More detailed analyses, which range from analysis of the trace to an automated identification process, enable determination of whether the object is friendly or enemy and allow the appropriate action to be taken. Current-generation AEW aircraft are, in general, developed from planes that have been flying for several decades, carrying out their task more or less efficiently. The type was designed to try and avoid the growing threat posed by hypothetical surprise attacks carried out by various high speed nuclear-armed combat planes, a general tactic of the seventies, although the idea of extending the radar horizon by mounting search radar in aircraft dates from the Second World War. As they are already airborne in a location unknown to the enemy, these planes offer an impressive ability to neutralise the threat, above all when combined with effective zonal air defence deployments.

### The naval environment

The first experiments with radar mounted in a plane with the objective of searching the surrounding airspace and detecting other planes in flight go back to the forties, although the first definitive results did not emerge until the following decade. The oldest of this type of aircraft still flying is the small twin turbo-prop E-2 Hawkeye, a design which was acquired by the US Navy and very successfully exported to countries like Israel – which has transferred some to Mexico –, Japan, Egypt, Singapore, Taiwan, and France, which deploys them in its navy's air arm, the Aéronavale, serving on the aircraft carrier Charles de Gaulle. Hawkeyes currently flying have little in common with the design that the American Northrop Grumman Corporation developed in 1964 as the E-2A. The current standard is the E-2C and the most modern variant is the Hawkeye 2000, the latest development of this plane, which can take-off from land bases and carrier flight-decks. The most recent upgrade is designated CEC (Co-operative Engagement Capability), which enables it to operate in conjunction with surface ships, to provide zonal defence against ballistic missiles.

As to the technology, it features an enormous radome on the top of the fuselage that houses the radar antennae, which rotates constantly when transmitting or receiving. The most recent version, which was demonstrated in

1997, has a Lockheed Martin AN/APS-145 radar that is able to detect, identify and track up to two thousand targets within a range of over five hundred and fifty kilometres, giving the systems operators inside the fuselage information relating to course, speed, altitude and IFF identification – whether they are friendly or enemy.

There five crew members, including two pilots. When working in the naval environment, the mode of operation is to fly to a point situated 320 kilometres from the aircraft carrier acting as base and then to constantly circle it at an altitude of 9,000 metres. In this position, the plane surveys aerial movements, transmitting the information obtained to the escorting warships or combat air patrols.

**The most effective**

Of the aircraft used in this role today, the most highly rated is the AWACS (Airborne Warning And Control System), a plane also known as the E-3 Sentry. It is used by the United States Air Force, and by allied nations such as the UK, France and Saudi Arabia, as well as the North Atlantic Treaty Organisation (NATO) itself, which has a fleet of seventeen manned by multi-national crews, to guarantee the collective security of its members. One of the most up-to-date variants of this flying radar, a derivative of the original plane, uses a Boeing 767-200 ER rather than a Boeing 707-320 as the platform and is in service with Japan. The Sentry has many important positive features and it was a vital component of the recent military actions which took place in Serbia and Iraq, where it was used to both control friendly aircraft, while detecting any response from the enemy. Another feature to bear in mind is the ability of its radar to scrutinise an area from over four hundred kilometres distant, whether over sea or land, and from ground level up to the stratosphere.

Initial evaluation started in 1975, with the first production examples entering service two

years later. Over the nearly three decades that this plane has been in active service, the original model has evolved, with many modifications and modernisations. The first models were designated E-3A and were followed by the subsequent B and C versions, while the seven planes received by Britain, and the four by France, were designated D and E, respectively.

The unit price of three hundred million dollars per plane is not cheap, but it offers substantial advantages. The most important are those determined by the AN/AYP-2 radar (-1 in the first planes) and modernised under the RSIP (Radar System Improvement Programme),

which enables it to detect targets with a small radar cross-section or cruise missiles in flight, all of this while performing in an environment saturated with electronic countermeasures aimed at making its work more difficult. The crew is composed of four men to fly the plane and thirteen specialists in charge of operating the fourteen SDC display consoles and the two auxiliary ADU display units, which use data supplied and managed by the IBM CC-2 processor. These operators can cover surveillance, identification, arms control, battlefield direction and communications support missions.

Its operating range is substantial, as it can

carry out 6 hour-long patrol missions, after having first flown 1,610 km from its base. The latest models to be delivered include an aerial refuelling probe that allows the time spent on patrol to be increased to eleven hours.

## Other choices

Market expectation has led to the development of other options, some very complex, others more modest, thereby enabling the widest range of possible customers to be satisfied. One of the most modern is the one developed under the Australian Wedgetail programme, which is an AEW-C (Airborne Early Warning and Control) system with a fixed antenna, installed on a Boeing 737-700 airliner. Four units were purchased in December, 2000, with options on two more taken up in 2004. The revised delivery schedule anticipates the first two being received in November 2006. Its most distinctive feature is the radar, a Northrop Grumman ESSD MESA-type (Multi-role Electronically Scanned Array), with an immobile, fixed radome which carries out electronic sweeps, thereby eliminating problems associated with movement, and enabling contacts to be more precisely located. Its coverage is a constant 360° due to its rotating search beam, which operates in the L frequency band, and the identifier is included in the same antenna, thereby saving weight and making correlating the targets easier.

These advantages, which will probably be incorporated in future designs, led the Turks to choose this Boeing configuration. This purchase requires the investment of one thousand million dollars in four aircraft, for delivery starting in 2006, although changed economic circumstances in Turkey could lead to the whole project being abandoned.

A project which has successfully seen the light of day is the Argus light system, a Swedish AEW & C development of the small Saab 340B turboprop transport, designated S100B. Its main advantage lies in the fact that its Erieye radar antenna, made by Ericsson Microwave Systems, is flat and is fixed to the top of the fuselage, giving it 160° coverage on either

side. It can detect targets in flight or on the surface and its maximum range is said to be between 300 and 400 kilometres.

This interesting performance, linked with an equally interesting price, has meant that six have been sold to the Swedish air force, four to Greece – mounted on an Embraer RJ-145 aircraft –, and another four to Brazil, which uses them to monitor Amazonia.

The Israeli Phalcon AEWC & C (Airborne Early Warning Command and Control) system is more complicated than the planes already mentioned. In 2004, it made headlines in the newspapers when a deal was agreed to sell three to India with US approval – mounted on Ilyushin II-76 transports. A similar deal with China was blocked in 2000 following intense US pressure. The system is made in Israel by Elta, and one has already been supplied to Chile, mounted on a Boeing 707 and designated Condor. Other units, of which two at least

are fitted to Boeing 767 cells, are in service with Israel, but they are extremely secretive regarding exactly which equipment they link with it and how they use its performance. The Phalcon's most visible distinctive feature is its use of an ESA type radar with flat antennae, one on either side of the fuselage and another in a radome fixed to the nose. The Soviets and, subsequently, the Russians also value designs of this type. Earliest references relate to the Tupolev Tu-126 Moss, which mounted a rotating antenna on the fuselage of a Tu-114 airliner that was based on the Tu-95 Bear bomber and which served until the early eighties. The most recent is the Beriev A-50 Mainstay system, fitted to an Ilyushin 76MD transport plane. Sixteen of these aircraft have been built, including the latest A-50U version, fitted with the Schmel M rotating radar, which is able to track around five hundred targets simultaneously. A very similar model was demonstrated

by the Iraqis in the early 1990s, modified locally by them and designated Adnan 1, although its real capabilities were unknown and the two surviving planes were evacuated to Iran before the Coalition attack in 2003 and it is not known whether they are in operable condition. Lastly, it is worth noting that a lighter AEW system has also been designed, which can be fitted to a specially modified SH-3 Sea King helicopter. It is based on the Searchwater radar and has been in service with the UK since 1979. It was the only AEW system British forces were able to use in the Falklands War. Two of these helicopters, now upgraded with the Searchwater 2000 radar, collided and were destroyed during the military action in Iraq in 2003. Spain has received three examples, which make up its airborne warning network and are deployed in advance of any movement by the task force led by the fleet flagship, the aircraft carrier Principe de Asturias.

▲ *The Hawkeye 2000 is the latest development of the US Navy's AEW. One of its distinguishing details is the high number of blades on the new propellers.*

| Technical details: E-2C Hawkeye | |
|---|---|
| **Cost (in millions of dollars):** | 200 |
| **Size:** | |
| Length | 24,56 m |
| Height | 5,58 m |
| Wingspan | 17,60 m |
| Wing area | 65,03 m² |
| Flap area | 11,03 m² |
| Radome diameter | 7,32 m |
| **Weight:** | |
| Empty | 18.364 kg |
| Maximum | 24.689 kg |
| Internal fuel | 7.000 l |
| **Engines:** | Two Allison T56-A-427 turboprops of 5,100 horsepower each |
| **Performance:** | |
| Ceiling | 11.278 m |
| Maximum speed | 626 km/h |
| Cruising speed | 480 km/h |
| Take-off requirement | 564 m |
| Operating range | 320 km flight from base and 4 hours searching |
| Tranfer range | 2.854 km |

# JOINT STARS
## SURVEILLANCE AND TARGET-TRACKING

The recent conflicts in Iraq and Afghanistan, along with the Gulf War in 1991 and the attacks in Bosnia-Herzegovina in 1996, are just some of the situations where the E-SC Joint Stars aircraft of the US Air Force have been deployed.

These are specially modified airliners, sheltered by the obscurity of the night, which are equipped with sensors capable of observing what occurs on the ground, even when the targets are moving.

### Slow development

In the early 1970s, military operations in Vietnam showed the difficulty of tracking enemy movements at the time, above all when ground forces moved at night or in the jungle.

In the early 1980s, this problem was confron-

ted by a joint programme of the United States Air Force and the United States Army, who planned the development of a radar system to be used for surveillance and targeting, and which was assigned the initials J-STARS (Joint Surveillance and Target Attack Radar System).

The basic requirements stipulated that it should be able to detect, locate, identify, classify and track hostile targets moving on the ground in any atmospheric conditions and from a safe distance, and which would permit total survivability in the face of

anti-aircraft defences. Several projects were studied in order to evaluate the proposals made by industry, although it was not until 1985 that the solution presented by Grumman Melbourne Systems Division was chosen, a system which was initially designated EC-18C and later became E-8A.

The Boeing 707-300, the same plane that was being used for the AWACS airborne warning aircraft, was chosen as the airborne platform for the sensors and equipment. A series of modular ground-based stations, as proposed by Motorola for a previous design, were also

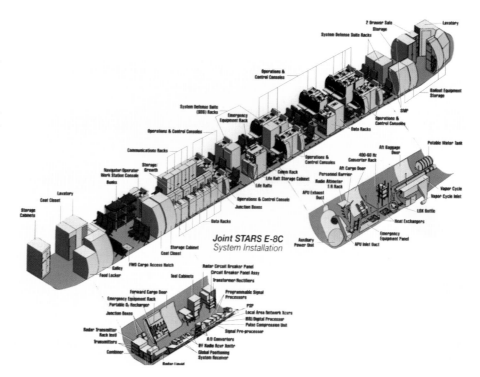

Joint STARS E-8C
System Installation

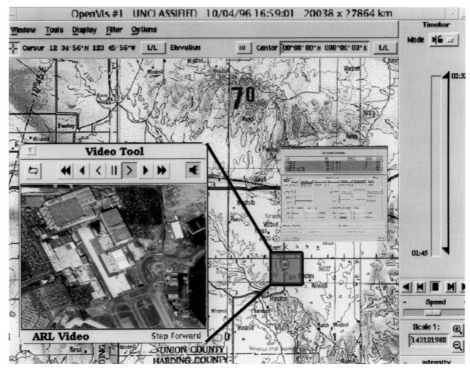

chosen, and received the designation GSM (Ground Station Modules).

The first prototype, using the body cell of a plane used by an airline, entered production at the end of July, 1987, and the second one was started in the autumn of 1988. The first flight tests took place on 22nd December of the same year.

Anticipated sales were for an order of twenty-two planes and a hundred ground stations,

which spurred the makers on to speed up the trials.

It was even decided to deploy the two prototypes to the Persian Gulf to participate in Operation Desert Storm.

Although they were supported by technicians and other non-military personnel, the truth was they performed excellently, which helped speed their incorporation into active service.

Their operational use resulted in missions lasting more than fourteen hours without a break, making use of their ability to refuel in flight, and they proved ideal in locating Iraqi batteries, including the fearsome surface-to-surface Scud missiles.

**The current contract**

This performance resulted in an initial production contract drawn up on 24th April, 1992,

and amended in May, 1993. The construction of a further six planes, in addition to the three prototypes already authorised, was agreed, including an upgraded variant designated the E-8C that had been requested in November 1990. This version entered service in 1996 and deliveries were made to the 116th Air Control Wing, based at Robins Air Force Base in Georgia, currently home to all seventeen aircraft, the last of which was delivered on 23rd March, 2005. In the long term, with its useful service life being prolonged until 2025, it is planned that the E-10 will, at first, complement, and then, replace, this aircraft. The E-10 is intended to merge the capabilities of the E-8, the AWACS, and other aircraft dedicated to Command and Control activities.

While the specification of this future aircraft is decided, the E-8C continues to be a fundamental pillar of US capabilities, the current version being the Block 20. Its most important feature is a twelve-metre long radome fitted to the bottom of the front of the fuselage and housing a radar able to produce a 120° directional beam that can sweep an area of 50,000 square kilometres in a short space of time. It is even able to find targets situated more than two hundred and fifty kilometres away, which says a lot for its performance and which, to date, remains unequalled.

Its defining sensor is none other than a multimode Westinghouse Norden AN/APY-3 SLAR (Side-Looking Phased-Array Radar). It operates in the I-band and includes a Moving Target Indicator (MTI). It functions connected to a set of image processors and powerful computers that handle the data received and present it on a total of eighteen Raytheon Model AXP-300/500 work-stations.

These positions are manned by the operators, who control the workings of the whole system and send out the information to other aircraft, to the ground stations, or to C4I hubs (Command, Control, Communications, Computers, and Intelligence) in real-time and encrypted. Using these capabilities, which were undreamed of only a few years ago, the enemy's movements and the position of opposing columns are known and the appropriate operations can be planned for their elimination.

The crew of the Joint-Stars is made up of twenty-one people, three pilots and eighteen operators although in long-endurance missions the crew can reach thirty-four, with six beds being available for rest. Flying at ten thousand metres altitude, the plane can overfly an area of a million square kilometres, almost twice the size of the Iberian peninsular, in eight hours.

The plane is able to discriminate between targets by analysing Doppler shifts and can identify whether vehicles have wheels or tracks or are armoured or not, or if the targets are helicopters or fixed-wing aircraft. The Synthetic Aperture Radar (SAR) mode enables it to concentrate the search beam on a small area to obtain very much more precise information and photographic-quality images.

| Technical details: E-8C JOINT STARS | |
|---|---|
| Cost (in millions of dollars): | 244,4 |
| **Size:** | |
| Length | 46,61 m |
| Height | 12,95 m |
| Wingspan | 44,42 m |
| **Weight:** | |
| Empty | 77.564 kg |
| Maximum | 152.407 kg |
| Internal fuel | 87.565 l |
| **Engines:** | 4 Pratt & Whitney JT3D-3B turbines with 8,500 kg thrust each |
| **Performance:** | |
| Ceiling | 12.802 m |
| Maximum speed | 0,8 Mach |
| Mission endurance | 11 hours maximum, can be extended to 20 with in-flight refuelling. |
| Maximum range | 9.000 km |
| Capability | to cover one million km² in an 8 hour flight |

# PILOTLESS AIRBORNE
## DEVICES

The European EADS consortium is also testing various designs. One of the most interesting is the Orka 1200, a vertical take-off device which can carry an optronic sensor and radar.

The Israelis have a long-standing tradition in the manufacture and sale of these devices. One of their most recent designs is the Hermes 180. These aircraft are especially useful in their fight against terrorism.

The availability of advanced technologies, and the desire of the military to be able to rely on a tool to carry out various missions without risking lives, as well as other factors, has led to the birth of a new family of pilotless remote-controlled aircraft, or ones capable of working independently.

These machines, which are generally known collectively as UAV (Unmanned Aerial Vehicles), are aircraft of varying sizes, depending on type and mission, which are used to obtain information about different targets and to transmit the data captured to their own control stations, or to other aircraft, cheaply and efficiently. In addition, their role has recently evolved, so that they are becoming platforms which are beginning to have the capacity to fire weapons at ground targets or to act as mobile stations for data transmission and other tasks.

## General acceptance

The current generation of UAV and their UCAC (Unmanned Combat Aerial Vehicles) derivatives were developed to respond to defined needs, although this evolution took place over a long period of time. The first references to this type of system were made in the 1950s, when the Teledyne Ryan 24 Firebee entered service. These were used for reconnaissance over Cuba and on electronic interference missions and the dropping of propaganda – psychological warfare – in favour of US intervention during the Vietnam War.

As time went by, it was the Israelis who concentrated on these types of measures, and developed them to realise their maximum

potential in military operations. One of their most remarkable missions was to send several of these aircraft over Syrian positions in the Berkaa Valley, where the Syrians based anti-aircraft batteries to defend their incursion into Lebanon. When they were illuminated by the air defence radars, details of the frequencies were transmitted to their control stations, which enabled the Israelis to evade the defensive threat and destroy the batteries with an air-strike.

They were also widely used in the invasion of the Lebanon in 1982, providing vital, real-time information about Israeli targets. The South Africans were the first among other countries to adopt this technology and test it in combat,

using vehicles based on civilian technology to direct their incursions into Angola. The Americans first began to use them in quantity during the Kuwaiti campaign in 1991 and during Operation Desert Storm. Results were so positive that many designs were drawn up during the 1990s, encouraged by the ever increasing needs that armies felt UAVs could satisfy.

## Similar designs

This type of machine can be divided into tactical and strategic types.

The first are those which are used in a specific situation in a restricted area or on the battlefield. The second, which have a much

greater range of up to thousands of kilometres, usually function fairly independently, although following previously defined search criteria.

Most of today's UAV consist of an aircraft powered by a piston or jet engine, although there are some with rotors which take off vertically and move horizontally, and even some battery or solar-powered models. Size depends on the load they are required to carry and the range expected of them. Tactical models are normally carried in medium-sized trucks and there are some very small ones which can be carried, disassembled, in a back-pack.

The operator is in charge of handling them,

using equipment of varying size to control them from a distance and to display the images supplied by the on-board sensors. It is fairly widespread practice to install this control centre in a container mounted on a vehicle for mobility.

The most-important factor of these machines is their payload, the systems that they can carry.

Their normal payload is television and video cameras for daytime operations and optronic systems for night vision, although there are some which are equipped with search radars and electronic disruption gear. Some can carry anti-tank missiles such as the Hellfire, and some have even been desig-

ned to carry an explosive charge that is precision-guided to impact on and destroy targets.

They have also been used to carry a laser illuminator which indicates the target another aircraft will attack, thereby avoiding the inherent risk involved in this role, especially where accuracy makes it necessary to get close to the target.

These devices work in a very simple way. They are assembled at the control point, the engines are switched on, and they are launched, with the route they are required to take to complete the mission having been pre-loaded in their navigation systems. They tend to fly high up to avoid being spotted

because of their noise, although there are others which move close to the ground to make it difficult for radars to pick them up. In the operating phase, they carry out the planned mission, which could be watching people trying to enter an area illegally or obtaining accurate images of military bases or of high-value installations.

### A model for every need

In recent times, the American RQ-1/MQ-1 Predator system has become well known. It normally flies at a medium altitude to carry out long range missions, recording information on especially important targets or trying to spot specific individuals.

Its use in the Afghan conflict in 2002 enabled its suitability as a weapons platform to be tested. To do so, a hundred and fifty anti-tank missiles were used to attack various targets with great precision.

Its wing-span is 14.8 m, which gives an idea of its size, while its range is close to 800 kilometres. The Global Hawk is much bigger, having a wing-span of 35.3 m, and a range of 15,000 km. For example, it can fly to a point 1,800 km away and then stay on patrol there for twenty-four hours before returning to its point of departure.

Both these systems are of a strategic nature and have already interested other countries, with Italy having decided to buy the former

and Australia the latter, and they are in direct competition with other less capable designs, costing considerably less. The Israelis, in the form of IAI (Israeli Aircraft Industries) or ELTA, offer such well-proven designs as the Searcher, Heron, Harpy or Hunter, some of which have already been used operationally for more than eighty thousand hours. The Searcher is a tactical model, the Heron can obtain strategic data, the Harpy guides itself into radars to destroy them, while the Hunter has been successfully ordered by the United States Army.

For its part, the United States Navy have adopted the RQ-2A Pioneer, which has had some important operating successes in the

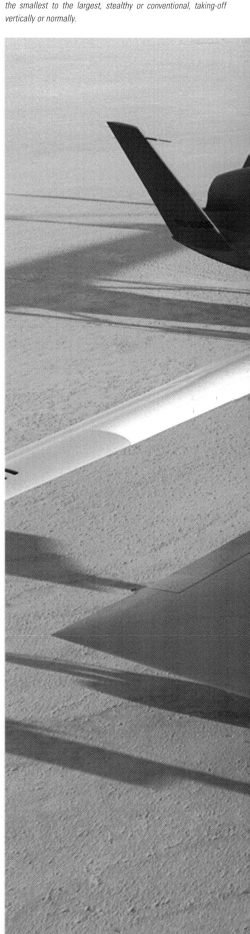

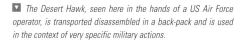

The Desert Hawk, seen here in the hands of a US Air Force operator, is transported disassembled in a back-pack and is used in the context of very specific military actions.

This picture shows the evolution of different UAV designs, from the smallest to the largest, stealthy or conventional, taking-off vertically or normally.

ten or so years it has been in service. This will be complemented by the Mariner, a more complex design based on upgrading the capacity of the Predator to enable it to carry one thousand five hundred kilograms of sensors and weapons. Its advantage is that it will cost four million dollars, roughly a fifth of the cost of a Global Hawk. Europe is not being left behind either. The Russians have made widespread use of their PCHELA-1 RPV (Remotely Piloted Vehicle) in Chechnya. It has a gyro-stabilised camera and is mainly used for target-spotting and tactical fire-control. The French deployed the Canadian-designed CL-289 in Bosnia, but they also have their own designs such as the HUNTER or the MART, the latter being successfully tested in the 1991 Iraqi campaign. Other countries have also made the effort to introduce their own designs. For example, the Spanish have developed the SIVA (Integrated Airborne Surveillance System

in Spanish) and the ALO (Light Observation Aircraft). The Germans have designed the Taifun to support their ground forces and the Greeks produce the NEARCHOS. For their part, the British offer the PHOENIX, a short range tactical surveillance machine used for artillery fire control, and the SPRITE, a tactical rotor-driven UAV. Even the Czechs have demonstrated their own designs, such as the SOJKA II/III, which also interests Hungary. Sweden, Austria, Japan, China, South Korea, Turkey, Taiwan, Switzerland, Tunisia, South Africa, Italy, Portugal, Iran, Iraq, India, Belgium and Australia also have their own designs. Apart from those already in service, there are even more complex and effective machines under development in many countries, The US, for example, has already flown the Boeing X-50A Dragonfly CRW (Canard Rotor/Wing), and the Bell Eagle Eye tilt rotor UAV, both of which can take off vertically and hover.

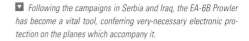

MULTI MISSION AIRCRAFT

Modular multi-purpose aircraft fitted for installation of numerous sensors, generic operator stations, data link and SATCOM

Performs a vast spectrum of missions:
- Signal Intelligence (SIGINT)
- Electronic Tactical Support
- Maritime Patrol
- Image Intelligence (IMINT)
- Airborne Early Warning & Control (AEW&C)

A powerful Ground Facility performs:
- Pre-mission preparations
- Post-mission analysis
- Intelligence extraction and reporting
- Real-time remote airborne systems operation and control

Air combat missions are mainly performed by fighter-bombers, which would certainly not be able to carry out their assigned missions without the support of other specialist aircraft. Of these, those of most interest are planes dedicated to reconnaissance and electronic warfare.

Countries that have restricted access to satellite technology entrust the task of gathering information on the ground to specially equipped reconnaissance airplanes. They usually have high-resolution long-range cameras installed in the fuselage that allow them to take photographs of targets before and after attacks, in order to evaluate the level of success obtained. Current technology also allows for the option of using pods, which can be installed on the plane's external fixing points and appropriately connected. They contain systems that are more advanced than the cameras themselves, ranging from radars to thermal-imaging equipment that which detects an object's heat in contrast to its surroundings.

**Emerging technologies**

The task of area and point reconnaissance, which is increasingly entrusted to UAV-type aircraft due to its inherent risk, has been the main task of many different aircraft, with the addition of the letter 'R' for 'Reconnaissance' added to their standard designation. By way of example, one of the most successful has been the RF-4 Phantom, a plane still serving with distinction in the German, Turkish and Greek air forces. Its most distinctive identifying feature is the housing underneath the longer, more pointed nose section, where the special photographic equipment has been fitted. It can capture outstandingly clear images from a safe distance, which makes subsequent interpretation of this intelligence easier.

This solution, based on now-obsolete technology, has one disadvantage, namely the time it

takes to develop, print, and interpret the film. To overcome this limitation, equipment such as RecceLite, made by the Israeli firm Rafael, has been appearing. This system was bought by the Spanish air force to give its EF-18s a new reconnaissance capability. Seventy per cent of its technology is based on the Litening targeting pod, which includes a new infrared system to capture digital images that can then be sent, via encrypted data-link, to ground stations for interpretation and distribution.

A similar concept is the TARPS (Tactical Airborne Reconnaissance Pod System), used by the United States Navy's Tomcats to obtain images, although its sensors are conventional cameras that record their information on a very long film. Other reconnaissance systems include ATARS (Advanced Tactical Air Reconnaissance System), which is in service with the US Marine Corps and includes two electro-optical and one infrared sensors, two digital tape recorders, an SAR radar and a digital data-link; Orpheus, used by the Dutch in their F-16s; and the US Air Force's TARS (Theatre Airborne Reconnaissance System), a reduced version of ATARS that incorporates electro-optical technology in the form of a 25 million pixel Recon Optical camera.

**Misleading the enemy**

Apart from the systems already mentioned, which are all dedicated to obtaining vital information on an enemy's positions, it is also necessary to have aircraft specialised in detecting and neutralising the enemy's electronic signals, as part of what is generally known as electronic warfare.

One of the specialised aircraft most commonly used in this field in the US armed forces is the EA-6B Prowler, which replaced the highly effective EF-111 Raven. Used by the US Navy and Marines, its most important ability lies in being able to create an electronic umbrella that protects its accompanying aircraft and specific ground sites from disruption of their systems by the enemy. It can also mislead the enemy with emissions designed to jam radar and communications. The procedure on these missions consists in flying with four ALQ-99 TJS (Tactical Jamming

System) containers under the wings, and with the USQ-113 system, which is a specialised communications jammer. It can also be armed with HARM missiles to attack anti-aircraft batteries.

The most recent version is the ICAP III (Improved CAPability), which is being fitted with the MIDS (Multifunctional Information Distribution System) that will enable it to send and receive data, via the Link 16 data link.

It is hoped that a replacement, currently called Growler, will be ready by the end of the decade. This will be a conversion to a new role of the F-18, including the installation of jamming pods under the wings. It will normally fly in formation with the planes it

is intended to protect and will use technology already tested by the EA-6B, as well as new equipment – for example the Northrop Grumman ALQ-218(V)2, and it will be able to carry five pods on its underwing pylons and under the fuselage.

While this new design is being developed, the task of signals intelligence falls to specialist aircraft like the eleven US Navy EP-3E ARIES II (Airborne Reconnaissance Integrated Electronic System), based on the P-3 Orion, which have receivers capable of gathering information and identifying radar and communications frequencies.

This data, suitably analysed, is used to design equipment to interfere with these frequencies and reduce their effectiveness to the

lowest possible level. Indeed, one of these aircraft starred in a recent international incident after being intercepted by the Chinese while flying an intelligence-gathering mission over their airspace.

The USAF RC-135V/W Rivet Joint is a similar, longer-ranged aircraft with sensors that can detect, identify, and locate signals throughout the electromagnetic spectrum. It is based on a C-135 aircraft whose forward end has been modified by L-3 Communications to carry the sensors and which has been converted to allow up to twenty-seven intelligence and electronic warfare specialists to travel inside the cabin. It has participated in support of every US military operation since entering service in 1962.

# HUNTING
## NAVAL TARGETS

The nature of warfare at sea requires the ability to sink both submarines underwater and warships sailing on the surface. Weapons systems, especially designed with specific levels of performance, are used for these tasks.

Submarines are normally neutralised with homing torpedoes, mines and depth charges. In contrast, attacks on surface warships are normally carried out using self-guiding missiles in order to avoid powerful anti-air defences and to hit targets from over the horizon.

**A specific threat**

There are many factors which have con-

tributed to shaping the background to present-day naval warfare. The political events which have occurred in recent decades have prompted changes in the nature of the threat and in the strategies employed in dealing with it. This change in approach started to take shape many years ago. An especially important change in this field took place with the appearance of land-based, followed by

carrier-based, aircraft. Years later, these were complemented by the now-popular and flexible, helicopter, which carries out a wide range of tasks with great effectiveness. In the near future, there are also plans to use remote-controlled devices, and others which work independently, to evaluate, and even to take action against, naval threats. Another fairly recent conceptual change occurred with the entry into service of nuclear-powered submarines. The use of this type of reactor to power submarines gave them a huge increase in flexibility and furtiveness, as they no longer needed to raise a schnorkel above the surface to carry out the process of recharging their batteries. New ideas

and systems such as AIP (Air-Independent Propulsion), fuel cells, etc., linked to conventional engines, will, in the next few years, see a revolution in this type of submarine.

Aircraft and helicopters carrying specialist Anti-Submarine Warfare (ASW) equipment on board are normally used to neutralise submarines. The reduction in activity carried out by the Russian navy, which is no longer the enemy for countries such as the USA and the UK, has led to the adoption of a more multirole philosophy and the attainment of a greater range of operating possibilities. Despite this, hunting submarines and surface warships is not easy for specialist aircraft. They have to rely on their sensors – radar, optronic measu-

res, sonar, sonar buoys, electronic emissions detectors etc. – to locate them and to try and fix their position, calculating the margin of error and then acting appropriately. The second phase, which takes place once the target has been identified, implies using one or other of the weapons designed for the job, such as torpedoes, mines, bombs, missiles, rockets and cannon, amongst others, and trying to sink the target being pursued.

### Different targets

If what is being attempted is the sinking of a submarine, then different weapons are used, depending on how it is travelling. If it is on the surface, something that normally happens

only in case of breakdown or when there is no sense of imminent danger, it is possible to resort to unguided rockets, cannon and heavy machine-guns, weapons which normally inflict structural damage requiring costly repairs. A more frequent situation is to locate a submarine submerged, with the depth depending on the individual tactical situation (conventional submarines have a diving limit of roughly 300 metres, while nuclear ones can reach 900 metres), so more specialised weapons systems must be used, including depth-charges, mines, torpedoes or missiles.

Depth charges, such as the British Mk.11 model or the Swedish SAM 204, are containers holding a large quantity of explosive and a trigger which makes them explode at a certain depth, a factor which limits their use. More modern and advanced are the US Quick Strike, or Russian AMD and MRP 80 mines, which include a processor that deto-nates when it detects a specific signature, previously programmed in its memory. This signature can relate to details of a specific vessel, or class of vessels, with details such as the acoustic cavitation of the hull or the radiated noise from the vessel's power-plant, especially that of the engines and screws. There are also tactical nuclear mines that are activated in the area where the submarine is believed to be sailing, although these are only in the arsenals of a selected group of countries. Their detonation sets off an underwater pressure wave that acts on the structure of the hull, caving it in and resulting in the submarine's sinking.

Although these anti-submarine weapons are usually highly efficient when used by well-drilled crews against a less well-trained enemy, a more frequent situation is the use of guided torpedoes, which are highly capable weapons, have a reasonable weight,

and are very effective in a wide range of conditions. They are normally carried on the underwing pylons on helicopters or in the weapons bays of specialist aircraft. Their tactical use is simple: they are launched, their seeking head activates on entering the water and their motor propels them until they strike the target, thereby exploding the warhead. Western lightweight torpedoes are normally around 324 millimetres in diameter, while the Russians have a wide range that includes many calibres.

The most common models in service are the British Sting Ray, the French Murène, the Russian APR-2E, and the American Mk.46 and Mk.50, which are available in different versions and upgrades. These devices are all fairly similar with respect to weight (two hundred to three hundred kilograms), speed (forty knots or more), and range (normally more than fifteen kilometres).

## Attacking warships

Fighting naval surface units implies a certain risk in view of the variety of defensive missile systems they carry. These include light-weight, short-range portable equipment, medium range and area air-defence missiles. To this collection, must be added modern multi-barrel cannon systems.

Faced with such difficulties, aircraft must act using the different systems available in combination, whether torpedoes, bombs, or submunitions dispensers. Cheaper and more accurate weapons are entering service all the time, which means surface warships are facing more threats, irrespective of type, tonnage, displacement or role.

The most usual offensive option is the use of independent, anti-ship guided weapons. Their features, above all the great distances from which they can be fired, even up to several hundred kilometres, mean that the firing aircraft is very safe, with very little prospect of it being fired upon.

Nevertheless, there are different types of missile, depending on the type of target, or the means of delivery. Short-range mis-

Guiding the different types of weapons used to attack naval targets requires sophisticated equipment like the US Navy's LANTIRN navigation and targeting pod.

siles are normally used by anti-submarine or multirole helicopters and are attached to winglets on the sides of the fuselage. They are fired once a contact has been selected as a target, with the missile being propelled by rocket motor and guided to the target by the seeking head, which is normally radar or infrared homing. Their main disadvantages are that their range does not normally exceed 30 km and that the warhead is limited in size, with several missiles being required to sink a modern frigate, although one is enough to do serious dama-

ge if it hits a vital system. Among the models in service are the Aérospatiale AS-15TT; the British Aerospace Sea Skua, already used by the British in the Falklands and Iraqi Wars; the Norwegian Kongsberg Penguin, which is fired from American and Spanish SH-60 helicopters; the Italian Marte; and the American Maverick and Hellfire, which is an anti-tank missile with very limited capability. If greater range or destructive ability is required, more capable missiles are used that, in turn, require the use of specialist combat or patrol aircraft, although there

are some heavy helicopters, which can also carry them.

The best are reputed to be the French Aérospatiale AM-39 Exocet, whose reputation was made in the Falklands War, when it sank the British ships HMS Sheffield and Atlantic Conveyor, and which was also responsible for the Iraqi attack on the frigate USS Stark in March, 1987; and the American AGM-84 Harpoon, which is in widespread service. Others are the Swedish RBS-15F, the Russian X-31 and X-15, and the Kormoran, which is used by the Germans.

▼ *During anti-surface ship attack missions, the aim is to try to ensure maximum survivability. Flares are used to deceive ship-borne anti-aircraft missiles.*

**Photo credits**

| | |
|---|---|
| Airbus : | p. 44, 45 |
| BAE Systems : | p. 30, 57, 58, 59 |
| EADS : | p. 9, 10, 11, 12, 13, 33 |
| U.S. Navy : | p. 14, 15, 36, 37, 38, 39, 40, 41, 42, 43, 55, 70, 92, 93, 94, 95 |
| USAF : | p. 16, 19, 20, 21, 22, 23, 24, 25, 26, 27, 28, 29, 45, 48, 49, 71, 73, 74, 75, 82, 84, 89 |
| | |
| Australian Ministry of Defense : | p. 34, 35, 46, 47, 54 |
| François Robineau, Dassault Aviation : | p. 62, 63, 90, 91 |
| Boeing : | p. 68, 69 |
| Northrop Grumman : | p. 75, 76, 77, 78, 79, 83, 84, 87 |
| Remaining photographies : | Octavio Díez, Aermacchi, Avions Marcel Dassault, MAPO, Artur Sarkisyan, NATO, Motorota. |